Electoral Systems and Voting in the United Kingdom

Books in the Politics Study Guides series

Electoral Systems and Voting in the United Kingdom

Chris Robinson

Edinburgh University Press

© Chris Robinson, 2010

Edinburgh University Press Ltd
22 George Square, Edinburgh
www.euppublishing.com

Typeset in 11/13pt Monotype Baskerville by
Servis Filmsetting Ltd, Stockport, Cheshire, and
printed and bound in Great Britain by
CPI Antony Rowe, Chippenham and Eastbourne

A CIP record for this book is available from the British Library

ISBN 978 0 7486 2750 9 (paperback)

The right of Chris Robinson to be identified as author of
this work has been asserted in accordance with the
Copyright, Designs and Patents Act 1988.

Published with the support of the Edinburgh
University Scholarly Publishing Initiatives Fund.

Contents

Boxes

Tables

Figures

Introduction

Contents

Overview

Students of politics have been afforded the opportunity to research the impact of the various recent constitutional reforms that have been made in the United Kingdom. This chapter introduces the reforms to the various methods of electing representatives in the UK.

In the first instance, the principles and functions of elections are explored. These will provide the reader with a useful point of reference when assessing the various electoral systems that are discussed in the following chapters of the book.

Key issues to be covered in this chapter

- Previous calls to reform the simple plurality electoral system
- Anomalies in the UK voting system
- The Blair government's constitutional reforms
- The main functions of elections
- The main principles of elections

Background

As recently as 1998, any book examining alternative voting systems to the one used to elect the British House of Commons would have had to look abroad for case studies of how they operate in practice. Apart from in Northern Ireland, all elections in the UK used the first-past-the-post electoral system. Books on electoral systems would often attempt some form of comparative analysis in order to interpret the likely impact of such systems if they were introduced for elections to Westminster. Students reading such books would have to become familiar with the workings of electoral systems around the world in order to obtain a contextual understanding of the strengths and weaknesses of the voting system in their own country.

The first-past-the-post voting system has been criticised for decades. Attempts to reform it go back to the period between the two world wars. In recent times calls for its reform have become louder. But despite these calls there was no real movement on this issue at all until the late 1990s. The reasons for this inaction for the half-century following the end of World War Two are easily explained. In the 1950s and 1960s, Labour and the Conservatives alternated in power in a political system where regularly over 90 per cent of voters supported them. The issue of electoral reform was not on their agendas; indeed, the issue was not debated beyond the political parties. Apart from the occasional by-election upset, Britain's two-party system seemed as secure and stable as ever. Appearances can be deceptive, however, because despite this apparent strength, neither Labour nor the Conservatives could ever muster 50 per cent of the vote when elected to office. This lack of a popular mandate has been one of the main criticisms levelled at UK governments over the years. However, given the fact that no other political party could muster a percentage of votes even in double figures during this era, this issue was not as controversial as it would become by the 1970s and 1980s.

Changes in voting behaviour

Over the past thirty years, there has been much to comment upon about changing voting behaviour in Britain. The stability and the certainties that were apparent in the 1950s and 1960s seem to have been replaced by greater uncertainties. Governments can be elected with hundred-seat majorities and yet having polled fewer votes than in the previous election when they had a majority of only twenty. Political parties may be within two percentage points of one another, but one might have ten times more seats than the other. Political parties may pick up 19 per cent of the national vote and win no seats in an election. These are just some of the anomalies that have been thrown up by the first-past-the-post voting system in recent elections.

These anomalies, which became characteristic of the UK electoral system, have ignited calls for reform. They started in the 1970s when the first cracks in the Conservative–Labour domination of votes started to show. In the February 1974 general election, the Liberals polled over six million votes (19.1 per cent of the vote) and yet won only fourteen seats in the House of Commons. The inadequacies of the system have to some extent been exposed by the way that voting behaviour has changed over the past forty years. It can be argued that these inadequacies have always existed; it is simply that their practical manifestations did not catch the public mood until the injustices, such as the one alluded to above, became so apparent. After the failure of any party to gain a parliamentary majority in the 2010 general election, resulting in a Conservative–Liberal coalition government, voting systems are now being looked at with renewed interest.

Government responses

These calls were given a sympathetic hearing by the incoming Blair government. Since the general election of 1997, a number of political and constitutional reforms, including changes to the way that the UK elects its MEPs and the introduction of devolved government in Scotland, Wales and Northern Ireland, have taken place in the United Kingdom, and these have been accompanied by a variety of electoral systems in use much closer to home than those described in textbooks in the past. It is now possible to study the workings of these systems and examine the effects that they have on voting behaviour as well as the impact that they have on political parties and the party system. It is possible to look at these systems in a UK context and analyse their strengths and weaknesses without having to make extrapolations and assumptions from one political system to another.

Aims of the book

One of the main aims of this book is to examine the various electoral systems mainly within, but sometimes beyond, the United Kingdom. The first part of this book examines the main categories of electoral system. Chapter 2 examines the workings of the simple plurality system, otherwise known as first-past-the-post, currently used for UK general elections and local government elections in England. Chapter 3 examines a number of majoritarian voting systems, and Chapter 4 examines several proportional electoral systems.

Each of these early chapters will look at the principles of each system and how it works in practice, and where possible will provide a sample of the voting paper used in the election concerned. The impact of the system will be assessed as well as an evaluation provided of its possible use in elections to the House of Commons. There are also several case studies; these are largely drawn from the United Kingdom, but occasionally there is a study from abroad to further illustrate the workings of a particular system or an electoral system which does not operate in the United Kingdom.

The second aim of this book is to analyse voting behaviour in the United Kingdom. Chapter 5 examines the main developments in voting behaviour in Great Britain since the 1950s. This covers the so-called era of alignment when Conservatives and Labour dominated the British political landscape in terms of votes and seats in the House of Commons. The chapter also covers the later period of dealignment where increasing numbers of voters broke free of these earlier ties to the two main parties. The chapter sets the context for the remainder of the book because, as mentioned earlier, it has been the long-term shifts in voting behaviour that have exposed the inadequacies of the UK voting system. The calls for electoral reform have coincided with calls for greater autonomy for parts of the United Kingdom, and in answering these calls, the Labour government elected in 1997 offered not only devolution, but devolution with proportionally elected assemblies.

The remaining four chapters are devoted to studying voting for those institutions with proportional electoral systems. Chapter 6 will examine voting in the three elections to the Scottish Parliament. Chapter 7 will analyse voting in elections to the National Assembly for Wales. Chapter 8 will examine the results of the elections to the Northern Ireland Assembly since 1998 and Chapter 9 will evaluate voting in UK elections to the European Parliament.

These later chapters will attempt to answer some key questions about voting in elections using proportional representation. First, how do voting patterns compare between elections to the devolved assemblies and the European Parliament, and elections to the House of Commons? Secondly, are these other elections second-order elections, in other words are they treated less seriously than elections to Westminster? Which political parties have done well and less well out of the use of these electoral systems? Is there evidence to show that the use of one proportional voting system produces a different outcome to another proportional system?

The remainder of this introduction seeks to act as a reminder of the main functions and principles of elections.

Box 1.1 Election functions and principles

Election functions

There are four key functions that can be associated with elections.

Participation Elections provide citizens with the idea that they are involved in the process of politics. Voting is an active thing which is important to have in a democracy, given that most of the time people are very passive, being willing to let the elected representatives get on with running the country. It is a worrying sign that turnout in general elections has fallen so significantly in recent years. Does the use of proportional electoral systems increase levels of participation?

Representation The UK has a system of representative democracy. Elections are periodic and the day-to-day politics takes place in the House of Commons and town and county halls up and down the country. Elections are a crucial means of enabling national and local representatives to be elected so that they may take decisions on behalf of the people in their respective communities. One theme which is developed in this book is the extent to which voters' party choice is affected by whether they are voting in a general or a devolved election.

Legitimacy Those who govern on behalf of the people should have the authority to do so. Elections give governments and other elected bodies the right to take decisions, pass laws and make policy.

Accountability Governments and other elected officials should serve only a limited time in office before subjecting themselves to re-election (or retiring from office). Elections ensure that those who are elected to serve are answerable (after a period of time) for the actions they have taken and that the people can get rid of a government with which they are not happy.

Election principles

There are a number of important benchmarks against which any electoral system should be judged. By the end of this book it should be evident how effectively the electoral systems in this book match up to these principles.

In the first place there are some basic principles that it must be hoped is true of all elections in the United Kingdom, whether they are conducted using proportional representation or not.

Elections should be free and fair This means that there should be universal suffrage, in other words all adults should be able to vote. There should be regular elections. One of the features of all the systems except one is that the election times are fixed. The exception is elections to the House of Commons, which are regular but at a time chosen by the Prime Minister. Free and fair elections require a secret ballot and no intimidation of voters. Officials are appointed to ensure that elections are conducted honestly.

Elections should be politically free This means that voters and candidates are free to express themselves within the law. Political parties can organise their campaigns freely and hold meetings for supporters without political control of such events. The press should be free to cover and report the campaign, again without interference from the authorities of the state. The state itself should not put out propaganda at this time which might favour the party in power.

There are some other principles which may be somewhat more contentious. These are the ones that may be failed by one or more electoral systems and it will be useful to look for some of these issues when reading this book.

The electoral system should be transparent An electoral system should be easy to understand. If there are complicated voting instructions, this might lead to voters making mistakes or deter them from voting altogether. Voting papers should be clearly laid out. Critics of the 2000 United States presidential election claim that in some states, the ballot paper was so confusing in its layout that it led to thousands of Al Gore (Democrat) supporters voting for the far-right candidate Pat Buchanan.

Election results should be administered fairly, with all candidates being able to be present at the counting process. The election result should be accepted as accurate and no winner should be declared until reasonable disputes about the result are settled. Any disagreement about the result should be challengeable in a recount of the votes. If anyone suspects that there have been irregularities in the conduct of any part of the election, the results should be subject to a court challenge. A secret ballot notwithstanding, ballot papers should be traceable by the order of a judge. Judges should be able to declare elections void and order a new vote.

Clearly, most political systems aspire to live up to all these principles. However (as the US example shows above), some of these principles will not be met. How fair is the simple plurality system when clearly not all votes are equal? How transparent are some proportional voting systems? Have recent controversies surrounding postal voting called into question the rigorousness with which these elections have been conducted? By the end of the book, some conclusions about the various electoral systems now in use in the United Kingdom may be drawn.

CHAPTER 2

The Plurality System

Contents

Overview

The simple plurality system has been used in general elections in the
United Kingdom since the introduction of the secret ballot in the nineteenth
century. It is a very simple system in terms of its workings, but the effects
of the system have the capacity to confuse observers of UK politics. This
chapter seeks to assess the impact of the simple plurality electoral system,
the controversies that have grown because of the system and the views of
the political parties on it.

Key issues to be covered in this chapter

- How the plurality system works
- An assessment of the impact of the plurality system
- The implications of the plurality system
- Controversies surrounding the plurality system
- The views of the main political parties on the plurality system

The system explained

The plurality system is also known as the simple majority system. Most citizens in the UK know this as the first-past-the-post electoral system. It is used in elections most notably in Canada, India, the United Kingdom and the United States of America.

This system will be very familiar to readers in Britain and United States. It is most commonly used in **single-member constituencies**, although it has been used in the UK in some local government elections to elect more than one representative in certain districts. In usual circumstances, in single-member constituencies, the plurality formula involves voters casting one vote. The candidate who obtains the most votes wins. In two-member constituencies, voters have two votes and the two candidates who achieve first and second place win the seats.

This electoral system is easily understood. Voters are not required to express a relative preference for the candidates on the ballot paper and there are no complicated **quotas** required for the counting of votes. In Britain the elections to the House of Commons are held in 650 **constituencies**, each electing a single member. The same system is used in local government elections. By-elections may be held in individual constituencies in the period between general elections in the event of the death or resignation of an MP.

Essentially this is a paper version of a vote based on a show of hands. Indeed, up until the 1870s elections were conducted where electors chose their representatives in this way in a public meeting with voters being able to see how each other was voting. After this time legislation was passed to introduce the **secret ballot** and measures to combat corrupt practices.

Assessment of the system

The result of an election using the simple plurality system can be measured and analysed in two main ways: first, based on the result in each individual constituency and second, based on an aggregation of the votes in all the 650 constituencies to get an overall state of the parties across the country.

In reality, however, the only place where the number of votes

Table 2.1 Constituency results from the 2005 general election (Birmingham Erdington)

Turnout 64,939 (48.9%)

Simon, S. L. (Lab)	16,810	(53.0%)
Elvidge, V. T. Ms (Con)	7,235	(22.8%)
Evans, J. (LD)	5,027	(15.8%)
Ebanks, S. E. Ms (BNP)	1,512	(4.8%)
Hepburn, R .L. (UKIP)	746	(2.3%)
Williams, T. (NF)	416	(1.3%)

Lab majority 9,575

formally matters is at the level of the individual constituency. Here the result is arrived at by adding up all the votes for each candidate, with the official national result being the total of the seats won by the various political parties. Table 2.1 shows the results from one constituency in the 2005 general election.

The result in Birmingham Erdington shows that using the simple plurality system, the Labour Party candidate, S. L. Simon, won the seat, taking over half of all the votes cast. All the votes for the remaining candidates are effectively wasted. In the case of Birmingham Erdington, it may be some consolation at least that the elected representative obtained a majority among those who voted. This is not always the case, as can be seen in Table 2.2.

In the case of Argyll & Bute, the winning candidate was well short of half of the vote; indeed, those opposing the Liberal Democrat candidate numbered nearly two-thirds of the vote. In the 2005 general election, a number of constituencies returned MPs who obtained fewer than half the total votes cast. It does not require too much mathematical analysis to understand the point that a government can be elected with a majority of seats in the House of Commons, without necessarily achieving a majority of the national vote (when all the individual constituency results are added together). The 2005 general election saw a major reduction in the size of

Table 2.2 Constituency results from the 2005 general election (Argyll & Bute)

Turnout 67,271 (64.3%)

Reid, A. (LD)	15,786 (36.5%)
McGrigor, J. A. R. N. (Con)	10,150 (23.5%)
Manson, C. Ms. (Lab)	9,696 (22.4%)
Strong, I. C. Ms. (SNP)	6,716 (15.5%)
Henderson, D. Ms. (SSP)	881 (2.0%)

LD majority 5,636

Table 2.3 Results of the 2005 United Kingdom general election

Party	% votes	No. of seats	% seats
Labour	35.3	356	55.1
Conservative	32.3	198	30.7
Liberal Democrat	22.1	62	9.6
Other	10.3	30	4.6

Labour's parliamentary majority, yet nevertheless the party managed to achieve a 55 per cent share of House of Commons seats with just 35 per cent of the national vote. Table 2.3 shows the percentage of votes and seats and the number of seats obtained by the three main political parties in the 2005 UK general election.

The simple plurality system enables the formation of a government with parliamentary majorities on a minority share of the vote. This has clearly been a controversial aspect of the British political system. In the 1950s and 1960s this was not as contentious, since although governments were being elected with less than half the vote, they were within only 1 to 3 per cent of that figure. By the

1970s, however, the figure was between 6 and 13 per cent below this level, again leaving the system open to criticism, especially from those political parties that were being hurt by it. There is further discussion of the changing nature of voting behaviour in the United Kingdom in Chapter 5.

The effects on the parties

Since 1945, Labour and the Conservatives have dominated British politics. Up until the 2010 general election, only these two parties were able to form governments. Many political commentators attribute this partly to the use of the simple plurality voting system in general elections. Other factors such as **social class** and **partisanship** (see Chapter 5) for a long time made a major contribution to the way people voted in elections.

How can the consequences of the simple plurality electoral system be explained? A number of factors can be identified. The first concerns the nature of the single-member constituency in UK politics. It may be argued that there is a mindset among politicians, academics and some members of the public of the importance of the constituency-based MP. So much is this the case that it is doubtful that any reform of the electoral system would do away with this feature. However, the existence of hundreds of relatively small constituencies each returning a single member is a key factor in the distortion that exists between the percentage of votes and the number of seats that each party receives.

In all but two elections between 1945 and 2010, the government has been elected with a majority of seats in the House of Commons (admittedly a few of these majorities have been rather small). It is doubtful, voting habits remaining equal, that there would have been majority governments throughout this time if alternative electoral systems to the simple plurality system had been used.

In stark contrast to this post-war two-party dominance has been the relative electoral failure among many smaller political parties. The Liberals, now the Liberal Democrats, have failed to achieve the number of seats that their level of support in votes suggests it should. Not all smaller parties have fared equally, however. Parties such as the Greens have found it impossible to gain any seats in the House of Commons. Some smaller parties, however, have fared better. The Scottish National Party has, to an extent, used the electoral system to its advantage, by being able to concentrate on campaigning in a coherent and limited number of seats. The SNP only fields candidates in the fifty-nine Scottish constituency seats in UK general elections. It would appear that the Liberal Democrats have taken this lesson on board. Since 1997, the party has concentrated its electoral campaign on a number of target seats, and was able to more than double its seats in the House of Commons in the election of that year. Since then, the Liberal Democrats have increased their number of House of Commons seats in each successive general election. Indeed, their share of the seats in 2005 was their best result since 1923.

The argument over the impact of the simple plurality system on smaller political parties is complicated further when their performance in local government elections is examined. In these elections, smaller political parties have much greater success. The Liberal Democrats have political control of a number of large local authorities in the UK. Yet the electoral system used in local government elections is the simple plurality system, in other words precisely the same electoral system as is used in general elections. This might be explained by the existence of differentiated perceptions among voters when participating in different types of elections. In other words, people may treat different types of elections in different ways. Perhaps voters are willing to give the Liberal Democrats a chance in local elections. Indeed, once they have succeeded in winning council seats, voters may then no longer see voting locally for the party as a wasted vote.

Perhaps placing the responsibility on the simple plurality electoral system for the fortunes of smaller political parties is too simplistic. Whatever the reason for the differences in outcomes, it should be understood that an electoral system on its own does not facilitate an outcome. It is also important to consider the context in which the electoral system is used.

The implications of this system for representation and governance

There are three main consequences of the simple plurality system as used for elections to the House of Commons in the UK.

- constituency representation
- single-party government
- strong and stable government

Constituency representation

Many politicians and commentators consider **constituency representation** as being an essential aspect of the UK political system. This representation is accentuated in the UK by the particular workings of the simple plurality system which in the UK operates using a large number of small constituencies with only one MP each. This is justified because in the UK, the sovereignty of Parliament is essentially legal sovereignty. It is essential that the electoral system operates in a way that maintains contact between the people and the MPs who exercise sovereignty on their behalf. Indeed, it is probably unrealistic to expect any replacement of the simple plurality system not to include constituency representation. A cynical response might be that MPs will of course highlight the notion of constituency representation given that they are themselves at the centre of it in the UK.

However, given that the accountability of the government in the UK political system is through the MP representing his or her constituents, the link connecting MPs to voters should not be underestimated. The MP and philosopher Edmund Burke saw the MP not as a simple delegate of the people in the constituency, but as someone who must use his or her own judgement, which may at times differ markedly from the views of the constituents. An MP should, of course, listen to these views and attempt to deal with any problem that is brought up at a regular constituency surgery.

Any previous innovations that appeared to threaten this constituency bond have been handled with care. In the 1960s, the Labour government of Harold Wilson established the role of Parliamentary Commissioner, or 'Ombudsman' – an individual able to investigate citizens' complaints involving public maladministration. The decision was made not to allow individuals to deal with the Ombudsman direct. Wilson himself reflects on this parliamentary innovation:

> One of our big problems was the understandable feelings MPs might
> have if their constituents were to go straight to the Ombudsman for

redress, bypassing traditional parliamentary methods of scrutinising the executive. We provided that all references to the Parliamentary Commissioner [the official title of the Ombudsman] should be made through a Member of Parliament.[1]

Understandably, Members of Parliament consider constituency representation to be very important. A big question does exist, however, over how important this issue is in the eyes of the general public. The weekend surgeries held by the vast majority of Members of Parliament are visited by only a tiny fraction of constituents and a significant number of people do not even know the name of their MP.

It would seem that the fortunes of individual MPs are bound up with those of their parties. In the event of an MP losing the endorsement of his or her party, history has shown that very few have been able to hold on to their seats without this support. Eddie Milne, the Labour MP for Blyth, kept his seat after being deselected by his constituency party in the February 1974 general election, but in the general election in October of the same year, he lost it to the official Labour Party candidate. Certainly in the past, it has appeared that the party can overcome even the most loved constituency representative.

Of course, this does not mean that personality is not important in British politics. On the contrary, the bond that receives most media coverage is that between the voter and the party leaders. This has endowed the political vocabulary with terms such as 'presidential', where voters seem more interested in national personalities than those at constituency level. With the arrival of television coverage of current affairs in the late 1950s, politics is often portrayed as a gladiatorial contest between the party leaders, which obscures many local issues and all but the most colourful of individual constituency candidates.

The link between the MP and the constituent is a very important theoretical part of the UK political system. Despite the genuine flaws in the theory when examined in practice, it is clear that a replacement electoral system without such a link would not be realistic. Given the fact that it is the House of Commons (composed entirely of such constituency representatives) that would ultimately decide this matter, the possibility is even more remote.

Single-party government

Notwithstanding the outcome in 2010, British politics has been characterised by single-party government. In other words, this is where members of only one political party hold ministerial positions in the government. This certainly contrasts with many governments in continental Europe where **coalitions** of two or more political parties are not uncommon. The UK alone out of all European countries uses the simple plurality electoral system and it is not unreasonable to assume that this is linked to single parties holding power.

Since 1900, there have been only thirteen and a half years during which the country has been governed by coalition; eight and a half of those years saw wartime coalitions such as that led by Winston Churchill between 1940 and 1945. So in peacetime, only five of the past one hundred and eight years have been, in the words of the British academic David Butler, 'clear and explicit coalition government'.[2] Clearly, however, this figure is set to rise.

Certainly, the outcome of the 2010 general election may in future cast doubt on the single-party government thesis. Perhaps even before 2010, however, this thesis had overstated the extent to which single parties could govern without the help of other parties. David Butler has described a number of periods of government during this time which might have been overwhelmingly dominated by one party, but where there was at least the influence of another party at work. Table 2.4 offers a summary of his conclusions.

This table demonstrates that far from being defined purely in terms of single-party government, British politics was more complicated than this. There are many more years where the party in government, while not in a formal coalition with another political party, has had to accommodate some limits to its political freedoms in certain circumstances, such as the Lib–Lab Pact of 1977–8 or, more recently, John Major's reliance on the Liberal Democrats in the ratification of the Maastricht Treaty in 1993. It would appear that far from unhindered power being exercised, there have been occasions where UK politicians have had to partake in the sort of political horse-trading that they purport to despise in our European neighbours.

Indeed, given the nature of UK political parties, it is somewhat disingenuous to describe some of our governments as single-party governments. Certainly, the experience of the rifts within the Labour

Table 2.4 Governments needing the support of another party 1900–78

Period	Governing party	Other factors
Jul 1900–Dec 1905	Con	Conservative–Liberal Unionist
Jan 1906–Dec 1910	Lib	Liberal majority with Labour and Irish Nationalist support
Jan 1910–May 1915	Lib	Liberals dependent on Irish Nationalists
May 1915–Nov 1922	Coalition	After 1918, coalition dominated by Conservatives
Jan 1924–Oct 1924	Lab	Labour dependent on Liberals
May 1929–Aug 1931	Lab	Labour dependent on Liberals
Aug 1931–Sep 1932	Coalition	Government composed of elements of three parties
Sep 1932–May 1940	National	Conservatives have by far the majority of seats
May 1940–May 1945	Coalition	Genuine coalition despite Conservative dominance
May 1945–Jul 1945	Con	Caretaker government
Mar 1974–Oct 1974	Lab	Labour dependent on other parties not uniting to defeat them
Apr 1976–Mar 1977	Lab	Labour dependent on other parties not uniting to defeat them
Mar 1977–Jul 1978	Lab	With agreed Liberal support
May 2010	Coalition	Conservative–Liberal Democrat

Adapted from D. Butler (ed.), *Coalitions in British Politics*, Macmillan, 1978, pp. 112–13.

government in the 1970s and those that appeared to cripple the Major government after 1992 would suggest a single party may be nominally in power but the factions within it appear to want to take it in different directions.

Strength and stability

Another feature of the British political system which has been, in part, ascribed to its electoral system has been its strong and stable nature. As mentioned above in the section on single-party government, there have been few coalition governments in the UK. It may be argued that coalitions effectively hobble governments in a manner that precludes strength.

Britain has had only eight main phases of government since 1945 (with thirteen prime ministers). This contrasts with countries such as Italy, which has had over fifty governments since the end of the Second World War. Such rapid turnover of governments has proved to be a real obstacle for governments wishing to enact their electoral programmes.

In Britain, governments last on average four years between general elections and thus there is relative stability in the political system. Governments usually get the bulk of their legislative programmes through Parliament, only rarely losing legislation in adverse votes in the House of Commons. The only occasion since 1945 when a government was defeated in a vote of confidence in the House of Commons was in March 1979. Stability, then, means regular elections at infrequent intervals. Strong governments are those that are able to carry out their manifesto promises by putting them on the statute book.

The difficulty with this analysis is that it is based upon a somewhat superficial understanding of the workings of the UK political system, not to mention those of many other European countries. Further examination of UK politics since 1945 reveals occasions where government majorities have been so small or non-existent as to make them vulnerable not only to the opposing parties in Parliament but also to internal divisions within the governing party. Four such periods were the following:

- February 1950 to October 1951
- October 1964 to March 1966
- February 1974 to May 1979
- April 1992 to May 1997

If a party attempts to govern without a House of Commons majority, it is said to be a **minority government**.

It may also be argued that the last two years of the Heath government did not display particular signs of strength and stability. Moreover, the final year of the Blair government was also weakened by events and a renewed Conservative Party. Gordon Brown, despite inheriting a comfortable majority in the House of Commons, was vulnerable to dissent and attacks from within his own party. Indeed, he narrowly avoided being challenged for the Labour Party leadership after some high-profile Cabinet resignations in June 2009.

In the main, the UK should be seen as having a stable political system, normally with strong governments. For around fifteen years since 1945, this has not been the case.

A stable political system is one to which most states would aspire. The merits of strong government may be argued, however. In Britain, most defenders of the simple plurality system would argue that political stability enables strong government and that this should be applauded as a virtue in the British political system. It means governments being able to implement a legislative programme. It is interesting, however, to listen very carefully to the proponents of this view. Consider the large parliamentary majority achieved by the Conservatives in 1983, which was justified by Conservative ministers and MPs as a means of carrying forward the Thatcherite agenda. In 1997, many of those same voices were attacking the size of the Labour government's majority for leading to the 'arrogance of power'. Conversely, members of the Labour Party attacked Mrs Thatcher's large majority after the 1983 general election whilst applauding Tony Blair's even bigger majority in 1997. What is clear is that strength only appears to be a virtue when one's own party is in office.

The views of the political parties

In the past, the main supporters and opponents of the simple plurality system have tended to cleave along lines of those that have thrived within the system and those that have not. Unsurprisingly, from what has been discussed so far, the Liberals (now the Liberal Democrats) have severely criticised the system. Traditionally the Conservatives have staunchly defended the simple plurality system,

Box 2.1 Controversies surrounding the simple plurality electoral system

It is certainly the case that the British electoral system is easy to understand. In any single-constituency contest, the candidate with the most votes cast wins the seat. That candidate becomes the Member of Parliament for the seat until the next general election. It has been argued that the simplicity of the simple plurality system represents one of its key advantages. There is no preferential voting, nor are there any complicated counting formulas.

Complications begin to arise, however, when all the individual constituency results are added up to arrive at a result for the general election as a whole. Some observers appear genuinely confused as to why a majority of seats in Parliament does not equate to a majority of votes in the country as a whole. The explanation is relatively straightforward: if sufficient MPs of the governing party are returned without a majority, then the governing party in Parliament (the sum total of those MPs) will not represent a majority of the electorate either.

Another phenomenon that often confuses voters is why after polling millions of votes, as they have done in every general election since 1974, the Liberals (now the Liberal Democrats) have seen so few of their candidates elected. Indeed, in 1983, the Liberal–SDP Alliance polled within two percentage points of the Labour Party and yet returned only a tenth of the seats. The answer rests on the nature of the distribution of party support across the country. Both Labour and the Conservatives have benefited from having support which was fairly well defined in certain locations, Labour traditionally polling well in Scotland, Wales and northern England in urban, working-class areas, and the Conservatives generally doing less well in these areas; conversely, the Conservatives have traditionally prospered in the south of England and in suburban and rural areas, with Labour doing much less well in these areas. The Liberals have very few geographical strongholds that they can rely upon. What tends to happen is that Liberals do reasonably well across large parts of the UK, amassing large numbers of votes nationally and often coming second in many constituencies. They do not perform sufficiently well in many constituencies to come first, however. Consequently, between 1970 and 1992, the Liberals/Liberal Democrats achieved only between ten and twenty seats.

The picture becomes even more confused when looking at other parties. In the October 1974 general election the SNP received nearly as many seats as the Liberals but with only a fraction of the vote. How may this be explained? The answer lies in the geographical spread of seats being fought by the SNP compared to the Liberals, with the former contesting only around seventy compared to the six hundred or more being fought by the Liberal Democrats. (Since the 2005 general election the number of Scottish Westminster constituencies has been reduced to fifty-nine.)

It may be argued, therefore, that for an electoral system which has the supposed merit of simplicity there are a number of confusing phenomena that accompany it. It is no surprise that these controversies have generated much debate both within and between the political parties about the merits of the system and the alternatives that might be considered to replace it.

although as part of the deal to form a coalition government with the Liberal Democrats, David Cameron is now promising a referendum on reforming elections to the House of Commons. This is in marked contrast to what he stated on the subject before and during the 2010 election campaign.

Since the late 1980s, the Labour Party has undergone a change of attitude about the system. Although there have always been many members who have favoured electoral reform (and those numbers increased during the years of the Conservative governments from 1979 to 1997), greater support for reform of the electoral system has become evident. In the early 1990s, the then Labour leader, Neil Kinnock, set up a committee to investigate the issue of electoral reform under the chairmanship of Professor Raymond Plant. The **Plant Report** proposed a majoritarian system as a replacement for the simple plurality system.[3] The problem for Labour was that it would need to win a general election in order to enact any reform and after losing three general elections in succession, many commentators wondered whether it could win again. This was certainly emphasised by Labour's fourth defeat in 1992. The party's recovery after 'Black Wednesday' in September 1992 and the reformist Blair agenda after July 1994 meant that it was increasingly likely that Labour's reformist credentials would be tested.

After the election of May 1997, the Labour government introduced a number of initiatives aimed at limiting the role of the simple plurality system and extending the use of alternative systems. In September 1997, there were successful **referendums** for devolved assemblies in Scotland and Wales, followed by legislation providing for proportional representation for elections to these assemblies. Since 1999, the elections to the European Parliament have been fought in the UK using a system of proportional representation. After the success of the 'Yes' campaign in the referendum on the Good Friday peace initiative in 1998, elections to the Northern Ireland Assembly are now also contested along proportional lines.

This approach has been criticised from a number of positions. Conservatives argue that reforms such as these are unnecessary and go too far in undermining the UK constitution. Conversely, many in the Liberal Democrats and groups such as the Electoral Reform Society argue that these sorts of reforms to the electoral system are typical of all British governments, offering reform for elections to institutions where no real power is exercised (indeed, Tony Blair did admit during the 1997 general election campaign that devolved assemblies in Scotland and Wales could be seen as little more than 'glorified parish councils'). While this argument could have been levelled before the establishment of the devolved bodies, few would now question whether they wield real power or make a difference to citizens. One could ask the question to those Scottish students whose financial burden is far lighter than their English counterparts. Indeed, in the wake of the Scottish government's decision to release the man convicted of the Lockerbie bombing, it may be suggested that the powers of the Scottish Parliament have developed in ways that even the most ardent nationalist would not have dared hope.

As Prime Minister, Tony Blair made early moves on electoral reform for elections to the House of Commons. He promised a referendum on the issue and asked the Liberal Democrat peer Lord Jenkins of Hillhead (the former Labour Cabinet minister Roy Jenkins) to head a commission to investigate and recommend an electoral system for elections to the House of Commons.[4] Lord Jenkins' report came in 1998 and received a lukewarm reception in Downing Street. For more details on the Jenkins Commission proposals, see Chapter 4. After the 2010 general election result, Gordon Brown and David Cameron both offered the Liberal Democrats the prospect of a referendum on electoral reform in return for this support.

The simple plurality system has survived for well over a century. The system is becoming encircled, however, with a growing number of bodies using alternatives, and if the second chamber becomes either partially or wholly elected then Westminster itself will become a home for proportional representation. This in itself might generate a major political storm as to which chamber of the UK Parliament has the greater legitimacy. The outcome of the 2010 general election makes the prospects for the plurality system more uncertain.

In the past, those who sought to defend the simple plurality system felt justified in shrugging off alternative systems as foreign or alien to British traditions. For the past ten years, however, many Britons have been using these alternative systems to elect their assembly members and MEPs. The systems have not led to catastrophe as some predicted. Could it be that the days of the simple plurality system, in UK elections to the House of Commons, are numbered?

· ·

What you should have learnt from reading this chapter

- An understanding of the essential features of the simple plurality system.

- A grasp of the main effects of the simple plurality system.

- A knowledge of the strengths and weaknesses of the simple plurality system.

- An understanding of what the main political parties think about the system and why.

- An assessment of why electoral reform in the United Kingdom has so far not encompassed elections to the House of Commons.

Glossary of key terms

Coalition A partnership of two or more political parties in government. This normally occurs when a single political party falls short of a parliamentary majority to form a government on its own. This is not the norm in British politics. In countries operating proportional voting systems, however, they are quite common.
Constituency The geographical district used in elections. Depending on the electoral system used, these districts may vary both in size and in the number of representatives to be returned in each.
Constituency representation MPs are returned from geographically

defined areas. Voters (constituents) in those areas therefore have a named individual (representative) to whom they may take their problems.

Minority government When a party seeks to govern without a majority of seats and does not enter into a coalition with another party. In such circumstances, the government is vulnerable to defeat in votes in the House of Commons. Between February and October 1974, and between 1976 and 1979, Britain had a minority Labour government.

Partisanship (also known as partisan alignment or party identification) A psychological attachment to a political party, which may vary in strength. It is more than simply voting for a party: it is argued that in the 1950s and 1960s, partisan alignment was one of the anchors of the stable two-party system.

Plant Report A report on electoral reform commissioned by the Labour Party. Professor Raymond (later to be Lord) Plant of Southampton University was asked to investigate alternatives to the first-past-the-post voting system. The final report was published in 1991.

Quota The figure, used in election counts, that determines the number of votes required to win a seat.

Referendum A vote taken on a question put to the people of a country. In Britain, there has only been one nationwide referendum, namely in 1975 on whether the UK should have remained part of the European Economic Community. There have also, however, been referendums in Scotland and Wales over the issue of devolution.

Secret ballot A ballot that enables voters to express their political preference in a manner which protects them from intimidation. In fact, in Britain, the vote is not technically secret. All ballot papers are coded and counterfoiled to enable officials to deal with any later breaches of electoral law which may arise.

Single-member constituency A constituency in which voters elect only one Member of Parliament to represent them.

Social class A classification which is usually based upon occupation. Broadly speaking, 'working class' refers to manual workers, and non-manual workers are normally referred to as 'middle class'.

? Likely examination questions

Outline three arguments for retaining the simple plurality system.

'The House of Commons should no longer be elected using the simple plurality electoral system.' Discuss.

Helpful websites

Sunder Katwala, *How to reform the electoral system*. The Fabian Society www.fabian-society.org.uk/publications/extracts/call-for-lab-libdem-deal-on-alternative-vote

Phil McKenna, *Why first-past-the-post voting is fundamentally flawed. The New Scientist*

www.newscientist.com/article/mg19826511.600-why-firstpastthepost-voting-is-fundamentally-flawed.html

 ## Suggestions for further reading

A. Blais, *To Keep or to Change First Past the Post? The Politics of Electoral Reform*, Oxford University Press, 2008.

M. Gallagher and P. Mitchell (eds), *The Politics of Electoral Systems*, Oxford University Press, 2005.

S. Henig and L. Baston, *Politico's Guide to the General Election 2005*, Politico's Publishing, 2005.

CHAPTER 3

Majoritarian Systems

Contents

Overview

One term used to classify electoral systems is 'majoritarian'. Systems such as these rely on candidates obtaining a majority of votes in their constituency in order to be elected. Given that, as seen in the last chapter, a number of seats in UK general elections may be won by candidates who obtain fewer than half the total votes cast, majoritarian electoral systems are seen by some reformers as the minimum needed to improve representative democracy in the UK.

This chapter will explain the principles as well as the features of some of these systems. In addition, the chapter will assess these systems and gauge the opinions of the political parties about their use.

Key issues to be covered in this chapter

- The principle of majoritarian electoral systems
- The different types of majoritarian electoral systems
- An assessment of the impact of majoritarian electoral systems
- The implications of majoritarian electoral systems
- Controversies surrounding majoritarian electoral systems
- The views of the main political parties on majoritarian electoral systems

Introduction

Majoritarian electoral systems are those in which the electorate return a representative with a majority of the votes cast in a particular electoral district or constituency. One of the consequences of such systems is that the government should also be returned with at least a majority of the whole electorate. As will be seen later in this chapter, this outcome is by no means guaranteed. Majoritarian electoral systems are not proportional, that is they do not produce a distribution of seats proportional to the distribution of votes obtained.

Advocates of majoritarian electoral systems maintain that by ensuring the return of representatives with more than 50 per cent of the vote, one of the main shortcomings of the simple plurality system is overcome. It may also be suggested that a majoritarian system is likely to be the least traumatic upon the working of the UK political system. For this reason majoritarian systems have some support within Gordon Brown's government (see below).

The first part of this chapter will focus on the workings of the majoritarian system in use in the UK, the supplementary vote, currently used to elect the London Mayor. A variation of this system, the alternative vote, currently in use for national elections in Australia, will also be examined briefly. Finally, there will be a brief study of the second-ballot system, which is used to elect the president of France. It is important to note at this point that the use of the supplementary vote in London does not extend to electing the Greater London Authority and it will therefore not be possible to analyse the impact of this system on the dynamics of London-wide representation. (The GLA is elected using the additional member proportional voting system and a thorough analysis of this system is provided in Chapter 4.)

The supplementary vote

As mentioned in the previous chapter, the commission of Professor Raymond Plant reported its findings to the Labour Party in 1991. Neil Kinnock had set up the commission to investigate alternatives to the simple plurality system. The report recommended a system called the supplementary vote, a variant of the alternative vote (see below). The report was quickly forgotten and the supplementary vote system went almost ignored for the best part of a decade.

The Blair government held a referendum in1999 to establish whether Londoners wanted an elected mayor and an elected strategic authority. The vote was carried overwhelmingly and the following year the first elections were held. As previously mentioned, the Greater London Authority uses the additional member system. The London Mayor is elected using a majoritarian system called the supplementary vote. In 2000 and 2004 Ken Livingstone was elected London Mayor and in 2008, Boris Johnson won the contest.

The system explained

The system works as follows: if there are more than two candidates who wish to stand, the London Mayor is elected using the supplementary vote (if there are only two candidates, the first-past-the-post system is used). The supplementary vote system is a **preferential voting** system. Voters may cast a first and second preference, indicating their preference 1 and preference 2. Voters are not obliged to cast a second-choice vote, but must cast a first choice in order for the ballot paper to be counted. If a candidate receives more than half the valid first-choice votes (in other words, a majority), he or she is elected.

If no candidate receives half the first-choice votes, all the other candidates except the two with the most first-choice votes are eliminated. At that point the second-choice votes from the eliminated candidates are added up and redistributed between the first two candidates. The candidate with the most first- and second-choice votes wins the election. The **redistribution** of these second-choice votes ensures that the winner achieves more than 50 per cent of the vote. The following flow diagram provides an illustration of how the system works.

In the event of a tie, the Greater London Returning Officer (GLRO) draws lots. No matter how close the result, a London-wide **recount** cannot be ordered – the GLRO does not have the power to do this. Only constituency returning officers in the London Boroughs are able to order recounts.

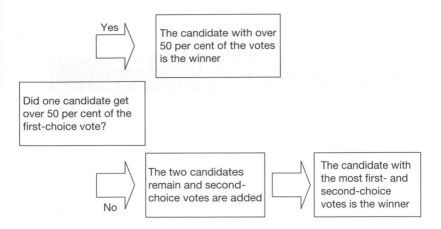

Figure 3.1 (overleaf) shows a sample ballot paper.

Box 3.1 Case study: the election of the London Mayor

Background

There have been three elections for the position of London Mayor (in 2000, 2004 and 2008) and all three have used this system. Candidates from all the main parties select their candidates to fight the election about a year in advance of polling day.

The Labour Party encountered major difficulties in the run-up to the 2000 election. The Labour leadership did not want the MP for Brent East and former leader of the Greater London Council, Ken Livingstone, to be the Labour candidate. Frank Dobson, the Labour Health Secretary, was Tony Blair's preferred candidate and he became the official Labour candidate for London Mayor. Ken Livingstone subsequently declared that he would stand as an independent candidate.

The Conservatives had their own problems in that their candidate, Lord Archer, was accused of perjuring himself in court in a case heard in 1987 in which he was acquitted. He too was ruled out of the race and was expelled from the Conservative Party. Former minister Steven Norris was drafted in to become the official Conservative Party candidate. In many respects the 2000 election for London Mayor was dominated by high political drama, with not much thought being given to the new electoral system that would be used. Figure 3.1 (overleaf) shows a sample ballot paper.

Election of the Mayor

Vote once (X) in column one for your first choice
Vote once (X) in column two for your second choice

		column one **first choice**	column two **second choice**
1	CANDIDATE 01 Party C		
2	CANDIDATE 02 Party A		
3	CANDIDATE 03 Party B		
4	CANDIDATE 04 Party D		
5	CANDIDATE 05 Party J		
6	CANDIDATE 06 Party I		
7	CANDIDATE 07 Party G		
8	CANDIDATE 08 Party F		
9	CANDIDATE 09 Party E		
10	CANDIDATE 10 Party H		

Figure 3.1 Election of the London Mayor, ballot paper

The 2004 Mayoral election was very much a rerun of that of 2000, with Livingstone and Norris in the end fighting head to head with all the other candidates eliminated. There was little of the intra-party political drama of four years earlier. Ken Livingstone had been readmitted to the Labour Party and stood as the official Labour candidate. By this time Tony Blair's popularity had been seriously dented by the Iraq war, and this may be seen as one reason for a decline in Labour support between 2004 and 2008. It is possible that it was Livingstone's own personal standing with Londoners at the time rather than any strong feelings for the Labour Party that enabled him to retain his position as London Mayor.

In 2008, it could be argued that the national political scene dominated the campaign for London Mayor. The unpopularity of Gordon Brown's government and the worsening economy combined with the feeling in London that someone else should be given a chance, all led to a stunning defeat for Ken Livingstone.

The results

Tables 3.1, 3.2 and 3.3 provide more detailed information on the outcome of the results of the elections in 2000, 2004 and 2008. The winning candidate in each election is in bold type.

As can be seen, in 2000 Ken Livingstone failed to secure more than 50 per cent of first-preference votes. The second-preference votes of those electors who had placed other candidates first enabled Ken Livingstone to become elected. It is interesting to examine the combined votes of Livingstone and Dobson. Assuming the supporters of both candidates were naturally inclined to Labour, one could speculate that had Ken Livingstone been the official Labour candidate, he might have achieved the 50 per cent plus needed to win on the first-preference count. Clearly, all of the other candidates will have received second-preference votes as well as the two that went through, but these votes play no further part in the election process.

The dramatic decline in Labour support between 2000 and 2004 is interesting. In 2000, 52 per cent of first-preference votes went to either Ken Livingstone or Frank Dobson. By 2004, with Livingstone officially Labour again, the party mustered only 35.7 per cent. The elections came at a bad time for the government, given especially the issue of Iraq, but the Conservatives did not capitalise much and saw only a fractional increase in support.

It is the smaller parties that seem to have benefited most from Labour's decline. This election was held in the same period as the European parliamentary elections, where parties such as the Greens and the United Kingdom Independence Party both gained seats. In London too they increased their share of the vote.

In 2008, Labour finally lost the battle for the London Mayoralty. This election was not fought against the background of Tony Blair and the Iraq war. A new Prime Minister whose popularity was falling dramatically and the incumbent Mayor whose own opinion poll ratings were low meant Labour was vulnerable. Add to the equation a resurgent Conservative Party and the scene was set for an upset.

Boris Johnson's victory was one of three Tory successes in the spring of 2008, the others being the Crewe and Nantwich **by-election**, where Labour lost a safe seat, and the big Conservative gains in the local council elections in early May. For the first time in over twenty years the Conservatives were looking strong ahead of a general election.

Table 3.1 The 2000 election of the London Mayor

Candidate	Party	First preference	%	Second preference	Total
Ken Livingstone	**Independent**	**667,877**	**39%**	**108,550**	**776,427**
Steven Norris	Conservative	464,434	27%	99,703	564,137
Frank Dobson	Labour	223,884	13%		
Susan Kramer	Liberal Democrat	203,452	12%		
Ram Gidoomal	Christian Peoples Alliance	42,060	2%		
Darren Johnson	Green	38,121	2%		
Michael Newland	British National Party	33,569	2%		
Damian Hockney	UK Independence Party	16,234	1%		
Geoffrey Ben-Nathan	Pro-Motorist Small Shop	9,956	1%		
Ashwin Kumar Tanna	Independent	9,015	1%		
Geoffrey Clements	Natural Law Party	5,470	0%		
Total		**1,714,072**		**208,253**	**1,340,564**

Table 3.2 The 2004 election of the London Mayor

Candidate	Party	First preference	%	Second preference	Total
Ken Livingstone	**Labour**	**685,541**	**35.7**	**250,517**	**828,380**
Steven Norris	Conservative	542,423	28.2	222,559	667,178
Simon Hughes	Liberal Democrat	284,645	14.8		
Frank Maloney	UK Independence Party	115,665	6.0		
Lindsey German	Respect	61,731	3.2		
Julian Leppert	British National Party	58,405	3.0		
Darren Johnson	Green Party	57,331	3.0		
Ram Gidoomal	Christian Peoples Alliance	41,696	2.2		
Tammy Nagalingham	Independent	6,692	0.4		
Total		**1,854,129**		**473,076**	**1,495,558**

Table 3.3 The 2008 election of the London Mayor

Candidate	Party	First preference	%	Second preference	Total
Boris Johnson	**Conservative**	**1,043,761**	**43.2**	**124,977**	**1,168,738**
Ken Livingstone	Labour	893,877	37.0	135,089	1,028,966
Brian Paddick	Liberal Democrat	236,685	9.8		
Sian Berry	Green Party	77,374	3.2		
Richard Barnbrook	British National Party	69,710	2.9		
Alan Craig	Christian Peoples Alliance	39,249	1.6		
Gerard Batten	UK Independence Party	22,422	0.9		
Lindsey German	Left List	16,796	0.7		
Matt O'Connor	English Democrats	10,695	0.4		
Winston McKenzie	Independent	5,389	0.2		
Total		**2,415,958**		**260,066**	**2,197,704**

Assessment of the system

In the previous section it was possible to chart the impact of the simple plurality system on the political parties, and examine constituency representation and the nature of single-party government. It is not possible to make such an analysis of the supplementary vote. The system is used only to elect a single individual (the London Mayor); the Greater London Authority is elected using the additional member system (see Chapter 4, section 2).

It can be concluded that the system does produce an elected Mayor who commands the support of at least half of those Londoners who turned out to vote. On each occasion, the winning candidate has required the second-preference votes of the other eliminated candidates' votes. Given the singular nature of the elected position, there is little room for advances by smaller parties. The best they might hope for is that their votes might be used in support of a candidate with not wholly dissimilar opinions and by implication this hinders a candidate who might be seen in hostile terms. In this respect, smaller political parties may have less direct influence on elections using the supplementary vote system.

It is possible to examine another majoritarian system that operates in much the same way as the supplementary vote, but this time on a country-wide basis. This may then enable a much more detailed analysis of the likely impact that a majoritarian electoral system will have on a political system (rather than just on part of one).

The alternative vote

The alternative vote has been a suggested replacement for the simple plurality system for nearly a century. The system was recommended by a **Royal Commission** during the First World War and was almost part of a deal brokered between the Liberals and Ramsay MacDonald in the dog days of his minority Labour government in 1931. A variant of the system was the recommendation of the Plant Report[1], which was commissioned by the Labour Party under Neil Kinnock (see above). Today the alternative vote is being seriously discussed once again.

The system explained

Voters receive a ballot paper with the names of the candidates and their party affiliation. Unlike the supplementary vote, voters do not only place a 1 and a 2 beside the names of their two most favoured candidates. Instead, they rank all the candidates in order of preference, with their most preferred candidate ranked number one, the second most preferred candidate numbered two and so on until either all the candidates have a number against their names or the voter wishes to rank only a certain number of the candidates.

The point of the system (like all majoritarian systems) is to ensure that the successful candidate obtains more than half the votes cast. When all the votes have been cast and the counting begins, the first task, as is the custom in most electoral systems, is to add up the total number of votes cast. After the total is added up, a check is made to find out if any candidate has polled more than 50 per cent. If any candidate has achieved this, then the procedure is complete and the said candidate is duly elected to the seat in question.

If no candidate receives over half the total of first-preference votes, however, the candidate with the fewest first preferences is eliminated from the race and his or her votes are redistributed to the candidate the voter has marked as the second preference. If, after this redistribution of votes, one candidate reaches the 50 per cent plus one mark, then that candidate becomes elected, otherwise the candidate who is now last is eliminated from the race and the votes are redistributed according to second preferences.

Complications

Supposing there are five candidates, say A, B, C, D and E, and no one polls over 50 per cent, then E, polling the fewest first preferences, is eliminated, with second preferences being redistributed to the remaining four candidates. What if, after this redistribution, there is still no candidate with over half the votes? Clearly, the next lowest candidate, say D, is eliminated and his second-preference votes are redistributed. The complication is that some of D's second preferences might have been cast for E, who has already been eliminated and votes recast. What happens to any new votes going to E? Clearly, E cannot re-enter the contest as his votes have already been redistributed according to the second preferences. Any new redistributed votes

Box 3.2 Case study: elections to the Australian House of Representatives

The Australian political system is based on a legislature comprising the Senate (upper House) and the House of Representatives (lower House), both elected directly by the people. The House of Representatives consists of 148 single-member electoral divisions. Elections to this House are based on the alternative vote system. The system is based on full preferential voting, and a candidate must receive 50 per cent plus one of the votes to be elected. A process of redistribution (as described earlier in the chapter) takes place if no candidate achieves a majority of votes. This process continues until one candidate does secure a majority plus one vote.

Australian electoral law stipulates that voters must express preferences for all the candidates on the ballot paper. If a voter only expresses two preferences (as happens in the supplementary vote, a variation on AV, outlined above), then the paper is classed as a spoiled one and is therefore declared void (which means it will not be counted in the result).

As with the system in Britain, the largest party in the House will normally form the government. The following figures, however, show that the result that one might expect from the voting figures does not actually materialise.

Australian election results

Table 3.4 shows the results for the Australian House of Representatives in the general election of October 2004.

The data shows that the Liberal Party held on to power. Nearly 12 per cent was added to their national vote to enable them to claim a majority of the vote and half the seats in the House of Representatives. Clearly, the first-preference votes alone would have been insufficient for the party to form a government.

Table 3.5 shows the results of the November 2007 general election result.

In this election the Australian Labor Party returned to power after more than a decade. Once again the party polled well short of 50 per cent of first-preference votes and it required the second preferences to gain the necessary majority of seats.

What the figures confirm is that the Alternative Vote does not necessarily treat parties in an equitable manner. If one looks at the Australian Greens, for example, it can be seen that in spite of finishing

Table 3.4 The 2004 Australian general election

Party name	First-preference vote	First-preference vote share %	Change from previous election %	Second-preference vote	Seats won	Seat share %
Liberal Party	4,781,313	40.81	+3.42	52.74	75	50.00
Australian Labor Party	4,409,117	37.64	-0.20	47.26	60	40.00
Australian Greens	841,734	7.19	+2.23		0	
National Party	690,275	5.89	+0.28		12	8.00
Independents	292,036	2.49	-0.41		3	2.00
Family First	235,315	2.01			0	
Australian Democrats	144,832	1.24	-4.17		0	
Pauline Hanson's One Nation Party	139,956	1.19	-3.15		0	
Votes for other than listed parties	180,554	1.54	-0.01			
Total	**11,715,132**	**100.00**		**100.00**	**150**	**100.00**

Source: Australian Electoral Commission.

Table 3.5 The 2007 Australian general election

Party name	First-preference vote	First-preference vote share %	Change from previous election %	Second-preference vote	Seats won	Seat share %
Australian Labor Party	5,388,147	43.38	+5.75	52.70	83	55.33
Liberal Party	4,546,536	36.61	-4.21	47.30	55	36.67
Australian Greens	967,781	7.79	+0.61		0	
National Party	682,424	5.49	-0.40		10	6.67
Independents	276,369	2.23	-0.27		2	1.33
Family First	246,792	1.99	-0.02		0	
Australian Democrats	89,810	0.72	-0.51		0	
Votes for other than listed parties	222,004	1.79	+0.25			
Totals	**12,419,863**	**100.00**		**100.00**	**150**	**100.00**

Source: Australian Electoral Commission.

in third place in both 2004 and 2007, they failed to pick up a single seat in the House of Representatives. On both occasions they beat the National Party into fourth place and yet the latter was able to pick up seats in the two general elections.

to E after D has been eliminated will be redistributed to the three remaining candidates according to the *third* preferences of E's votes. The process continues, redistributing votes upwards until one of the remaining candidates has achieved more than half of the total votes.

Another question about this system is what happens to those votes where no preference or perhaps only two or three preferences have been expressed. In such cases, the votes cannot be redistributed beyond the number indicated on the ballot paper, after which point they are removed from the counting process.

Implications for governance and representation

This system will tend to reward the candidate who is the least objectionable to most electors. In a sense, therefore, this system tends to reward the candidate who is the least unpopular, rather than the most popular. This hardly seems an ideal basis for representative government, in that the incoming administration will have less than a ringing endorsement from the voters. It may be argued, however, that under the simple plurality system, the scenes of triumph for the winning party on election night tend to mask the feelings of the majority of voters who, certainly in the UK since 1945, have found themselves not voting for the party that then goes on to form the next government.

It is important to distinguish the result at constituency level from that at national level. The alternative vote provides for candidates to be elected with over half the support in any single constituency, but this does not mean that the government will command the support of over half the voters nationwide. In Australia in 1954 the Labor Party won over 50 per cent of the national vote, but failed to win enough seats to form a government. This anomaly is due to factors that prevail in the simple plurality system. One party may gain a large number of seats with narrow majorities, while another party may win a smaller number of seats but with much bigger majorities. The resulting scenario is that one party outpolls another, but receives fewer seats.

MPs are elected with a majority support of their voting constituents. This is a very powerful justification for the alternative vote system, particularly in the light of the UK simple plurality system, where regularly nearly half of British MPs are elected by fewer than 50 per cent of the votes in their constituencies. However, despite each MP being elected by over 50 per cent of the constituency vote, there is no guarantee that the government will have the support of over half the national electorate.

Furthermore, as the data in the above tables illustrates, the system does not provide for a proportional result. Indeed, there is no guarantee that the system could produce a more proportionate result than the simple plurality system. The fact that many MPs in both the Labour Party and the Conservative Party prefer this system is an indication that the alternative vote is likely to sustain the current pattern in British politics, with most of its weaknesses and inadequacies remaining. Clearly, small parties are unlikely to see many benefits arising from the introduction of this system.

Another feature of this system is that it is based on single-member constituencies, which would effectively maintain the current arrangement. This is a powerful argument in its favour, given the strength of parliamentary feeling about the need to preserve the bond that exists between MPs and their constituents.

This is not a system which is likely to foster the rise of extremist parties. In this respect it is unlike some of the systems of **proportional representation** which do enable small parties, often on the far right or left, being able to wield influence far out of proportion to the support they command in the country as a whole. However, the result of this system would be the election of many candidates who were not the first choice of most of the electorate, with this potentially leading to representation by the least common denominators of acceptability to the electorate. Once again, this is hardly a ringing endorsement of representative democracy.

Finally, it may be argued that the system provides no real transfer of power to the electorate. The political parties remain very powerful in being able to select the candidates that are put before the electorate. As such, the most radical of reformers see this system as something of a compromise.

This system has been at the forefront of consideration for

replacing the simple plurality system for over eighty years and, as such, it has been subject to much scrutiny. In spite of its many critics, however, given the political situation following the 2010 general election, it still seems likely to be the voting system that is put before the British public in a referendum.

Clearly, this system is not intended to be a proportional one, and so one should not expect the sort of match between votes and seats that are found in a list system, for example. However, in a system the avowed intention of which is to secure majority rule, the evidence from this brief case study at least suggests that its shortcomings would be a focus of renewed criticism if it were introduced in Britain.

The second ballot

The second- (or two-) ballot system uses two ballots (normally a week apart) to ensure that the winner has a majority of the votes cast. A form of this system is currently used in France to elect the country's president. When the system is used for assembly elections, it is based on single-member constituencies. For further information on other countries that use this system, David Farrell offers a number of examples of where the system is used at one or more level of elections.[2]

As mentioned previously, the purpose of majoritarian electoral systems is generally to secure the election of a candidate with over half the votes cast. This particular system uses two ballots to achieve this result, although the contest may be successfully concluded for one candidate after the first round of balloting.

The system explained

In the first ballot, all the votes are counted and if one of the candidates wins over half of all votes cast, then he or she is elected. If no candidate achieves 50 per cent of the vote, a second ballot is necessary. This second ballot normally happens a week after the first. The candidates achieving the most and the second most votes in the first ballot will fight it out head to head in the second ballot, where the winner will be the candidate with the most votes (and will, by definition, have a majority of votes cast). There are some variations of the system which enable candidates to proceed to the second ballot having secured a certain percentage of votes. In such circumstances more than two candidates may find themselves going forward into the second round.

If one candidate is sufficiently popular, then there will be no need for a second ballot and he or she will be elected there and then. Given that in the 2005 general election in the UK, 47 per cent of MPs were elected with less than half of the vote in their constituencies, it is likely that a significant number of second ballot **run-offs** would take place if the system were to be used for elections to the House of Commons.

In the second round of voting, electors will have had time to make the decision about who they would like to see elected. This is not a problem for an individual voter if their preferred candidate in the first ballot goes through to the second. If the preferred candidate is eliminated then the voter has to make a decision perhaps based not on who they would next like to see elected, but on those they definitely *would not* like to see elected.

It may well be that the parties themselves will be on hand to provide advice. Perhaps a deal will be struck between two parties that in the event of either of their candidates being eliminated in the first round, they will recommend to their supporters to vote for the other party.

Whatever takes place before the second ballot, the result after it will result in the election of one candidate with over 50 per cent of the vote. In the case of parliamentary elections, given the unequal size of constituencies and the unequal magnitude of individual candidate majorities, there is no guarantee that the winning party in the assembly will have a majority of seats nationwide.

As mentioned above, in some variants of this system there is the provision for a run-off between more than two candidates. In such circumstances there is a distinct possibility that the overall winner will not have even 50 per cent of constituency votes, which rather appears to defeat the whole object of this electoral system.

Implications for governance and representation

The system provides for candidates to be elected with a majority of votes in the constituency. Furthermore it is easy to understand; voters can easily comprehend the notion of a 'run-off' contest.

Defenders of this system claim that the two-ballot process gives all

Box 3.3 Case study: French presidential elections

The second ballot system is used for elections both to the National Assembly (lower House) and for electing the President. There is, however, a difference in the mechanisms used for each of these elections. The rules for electing the President are very much what has been outlined above, that is a second-round contest between the two front-running candidates in the first ballot. The rules governing elections to the National Assembly are more complex, however, and provide for more than two candidates going through into the second round.

In legislative elections, candidates are able to proceed into the second round of voting if they have obtained a minimum of 12.5 per cent of registered voters (not of actual voters). Clearly, this ruling offers a greater chance to a larger number of candidates than pertains in the election of the President. While it is theoretically possible for up to eight candidates to go through to the second round (in the unlikely assumption that there is 100 per cent turnout and that all eight obtain exactly the same number of votes), more of these contests are between three candidates. Even this is not common, however. In French legislative elections in 1993, only fifteen such three-way contests took place out of four hundred and fifty elections (representing only 3 per cent).[3]

Table 3.6 shows the results of the 2002 French presidential election.

Table 3.6 The 2002 French presidential election

Candidate	First round %	Second round %
Jacques Chirac	19.83	82.14
Jean-Marie Le Pen	16.91	17.85
Lionel Jospin	16.14	
François Bayrou	6.84	
Arlette Laguiller	5.73	
Jean-Pierre Chevènement	5.33	
Noël Mamère	5.24	
Olivier Besancenot	4.26	

Table 3.6 (continued)

Candidate	First round %	Second round %
Jean Saint-Josse	4.25	
Alain Madelin	3.92	
Robert Hue	3.38	
Bruno Mégret	2.35	
Christiane Taubira	2.32	
Corinne Lepage	1.88	
Christine Boutin	1.19	
Daniel Gluckstein	0.47	

This was a massive result for the sitting French President, Jacques Chirac. The final outcome, however, does cover up some interesting politics. The main challenger to Chirac in the run-up to the election was former Socialist Prime Minister Lionel Jospin. He was beaten into third place by the far-right National Front leader, Jean-Marie Le Pen. Clearly, the vast majority of Jospin supporters, faced with the choice of voting for either the right or the extreme right, decided on the former and supported Chirac in the second ballot. The supporters of the other candidates, mostly radical, socialist, communist and environmental party supporters, did likewise.

Table 3.7 shows the results of the 2007 French presidential election.

In this election, the conservative Nicolas Sarkozy beat his socialist rival, Ségolène Royal, in the first ballot but failed to secure more than half of the vote. In the second ballot, the combination of Le Pen's far-right supporters plus those from other right-of-centre parties was enough to outnumber the supporters from left-wing groups. The balance of second-ballot votes therefore went to Sarkozy and along with it the French presidency.

It is quite possible for the forerunner in the first ballot to lose in the second, if there is a shift of support for candidates in the period inbetween. This was indeed the case in the 1995 presidential election. In the first ballot, Lionel Jospin came first with 22.2 per cent, with Jacques Chirac obtaining 20.8 per cent. Jean-Marie Le Pen came third, with 18.6 per cent, and was eliminated. In the second round of voting, Le Pen's supporters went over to Chirac and he beat Jospin by a margin of over 5 per cent.

Table 3.7 The 2007 French presidential election

Candidate	First round %	Second round %
Nicolas Sarkozy	31.18	53.06
Ségolène Royal	25.87	46.94
François Bayrou	18.57	
Jean-Marie Le Pen	10.44	
Olivier Besancenot	4.08	
Philippe de Villiers	2.23	
Marie-George Buffet	1.93	
Dominique Voynet	1.57	
Arlette Laguiller	1.33	
José Bové	1.32	
Frédéric Nihous	1.15	
Gérard Schivardi	0.34	

candidates a chance early on and enables voters to express a relative choice. According to this view, voting is not about absolutes; when given the choice, voters would prefer to opt for a candidate nearer to them politically, if their first choice cannot continue.

However, there is a need to prolong the process into two phases, over a week-long period (two weeks in some cases). Furthermore, it is a system that asks voters to consider switching allegiances should their preferred candidate in the first round of voting be excluded from the second round. Finally, there is no guarantee that a governing party elected using this system will have a majority of votes in the country, given that constituency sizes may vary and the magnitude of individual constituency majorities may vary widely.

Those who would criticise the second ballot from a British perspective argue that the system is totally alien to British voting culture and that the idea of expecting voters to turn up to vote twice in the space of a week would be asking too much. In 1974, there was a six-point reduction in turnout between the two elections in February and

October. The conclusion drawn from this observation is that people's interest in politics wanes if there is an overexposure to it in the media. Certainly the experience of the 1997 general election, where the turnout was only 70 per cent after a full five-year Parliament, is not encouraging in this respect. The elections of 2001 and 2005, with turnouts of around 60 per cent also raise further doubts.

The evidence of a fall in voter turnout is mixed, however, when examining the second ballot system in practice. Farrell indicates that during the 1960s, turnout dropped by over 12 per cent between the first and second ballot.[4]

Evidence from the French presidential elections in 1995, however, shows that turnout actually increased between the two ballots. On this basis it would be difficult to draw any firm conclusions. It may be that the critical factor in voter turnout is not the frequency of ballots, but the interest that is generated among the electorate. In the case of the French presidential election in 1995, the result in the first round was very close for the top three candidates. This might have ignited interest in the second round of voting.

· ·

What you should have learnt from reading this chapter

- An understanding of the principle behind majoritarian electoral systems
- An understanding of the different types of majoritarian electoral system
- An understanding of where different majoritarian electoral systems apply
- A grasp of the main effects of majoritarian electoral systems
- A knowledge of the strengths and weaknesses of majoritarian electoral systems

Glossary of key terms

By-election In Britain, an election that takes place in a constituency where a vacancy has arisen due to either the death, resignation or disqualification of a Member of Parliament or other elected representative.
Majoritarian A term to describe an electoral system the aim of which is to ensure that MPs are supported by at least half of their constituents. The systems do not guarantee that a government is elected with at least 50 per cent of the voters. The best-known of these systems are the supplementary vote, the second ballot and the alternative vote.

Preferential voting Rather than placing an X on the ballot paper, voters are asked to express their vote in preferential terms (1, 2, 3, 4 and so on). The alternative vote and the single transferable vote are examples of preferential voting.

Proportional representation Not a system of voting but a collective term used to describe an electoral system in which the proportion of seats that a party obtains in an assembly matches the percentage of votes that the party receives.

Recount When the result of an election is so close that an error in the original count could affect the final result, there may be an appeal for the votes to be counted again. It is not uncommon in very close elections for there to be more than one recount of the votes.

Redistribution In a preferential voting system, reallocation of votes if, for example, no candidate has achieved the quota necessary to be elected. Votes in excess of the quota may also be redistributed to other candidates. The alternative vote and the single transferable vote usually involve the redistribution of votes.

Royal Commission A body set up by the Prime Minister to investigate and report on a particular issue. These are usually chaired by a senior public figure (often a high-ranking judge or civil servant). The reports are made officially to the Queen and may become the basis of future government policy.

Run-off In the second-ballot system, if no candidate wins over half the vote in the first round, the top two candidates are involved in a second vote where one will win.

? Likely examination questions

Outline the workings of the supplementary vote.

What would be the main arguments for and against introducing a majoritarian electoral system for elections to the House of Commons?

💻 Helpful websites

The Electoral Reform Society

www.electoral-reform.org.uk/

House of Commons Electoral systems in the UK

www.parliament.uk/commons/lib/research/briefings/snpc-04458.pdf

Sunder Katwala, *How to reform the electoral system*. The Fabian Society

www.fabian-society.org.uk/publications/extracts/call-for-lab-libdem-deal-on-alternative-vote

Suggestions for further reading

D. Farrell, *Electoral Systems, a Comparative Introduction*, Palgrave Macmillan, 2001.

M. Gallagher and P. Mitchell (eds), *The Politics of Electoral Systems*, Oxford University Press, 2005.

D. B. Godley, 'The French General Election of 21–28 March 1993', *Electoral Studies*, vol. 12, no. 4, Elsevier, 1993.

CHAPTER 4

Proportional Systems

Contents

Overview

For some politicians and commentators, the majoritarian electoral systems discussed in the previous chapter are insufficiently representative and fair to all political parties. Proportional electoral systems, which attempt to match the percentage of seats to the percentage of votes cast for a particular party, seem to overcome such objections.

This chapter explores different proportional electoral systems and examines case studies from the UK and from abroad in order to provide a critical assessment of the workings of these systems.

Key issues to be covered in this chapter

- An explanation of how different proportional electoral systems work
- Case studies from the UK and abroad
- An assessment of the impact of these systems
- The implications these systems might have if deployed in UK elections to the House of Commons
- Controversies surrounding the systems

Table 4.1 The 2005 United Kingdom general election

Party	% votes	No. of seats	% Seats	No. of seats with PR
Labour	35.3	356	55.1	228
Conservative	32.3	198	30.7	207
Liberal Democrat	22.1	62	9.6	143
Other	10.3	30	4.6	67

The previous chapter examined three alternative voting systems to the simple plurality system which is currently used in British parliamentary elections. These systems are not proportional, in other words political parties would not receive seats in direct proportion to the votes obtained.

Some smaller political parties would be penalised by the introduction of majoritarian voting systems: indeed, there is no guarantee that a governing party would enjoy the support of the majority of the national vote. For these reasons, organisations such as the **Electoral Reform Society** and **Charter 88** have called for the introduction of **proportional representation**.

If seats in the House of Commons had been distributed in direct proportion to the votes obtained in the 2005 general election, there would have been no Labour majority in the House of Commons. Table 4.1 gives an indication of the actual result and how things might have been.

The Liberal Democrats and, to a lesser extent, the Conservatives under-performed in this general election. In the case of the Conservatives, their English vote matched their seats within 1 per cent (35 per cent of the votes to 36 per cent of the seats). In Scotland, however, the Tories obtained only one of the fifty-nine seats and yet polled over 15 per cent of the Scottish vote.

The final column of the table illustrates the outcome of the election had the distribution of seats been identical to the percentage of votes obtained. Labour would have been well short of the 324 seats it would have needed for a bare parliamentary majority. It becomes immediately clear that single-party government would probably not be a feature of the introduction of a form of proportional representation to UK general elections.

In fact, there has not been a single occasion since 1945 when a party has polled over 50 per cent of the vote. Even in the 1950s, when Labour and the Conservatives between them commanded as much as 96.8 per cent of the vote, the highest either could poll was in 1955, when the Conservatives achieved 49.7 per cent.

The difficulty with reading statistics in this manner is that one cannot simply transmute the voting figures from one system and then extrapolate an outcome using a different one. First, there is no guarantee that electors would cast their vote in the same way if a different system were to be used. Faced with a preferential voting system, for example, it is quite possible that some voters would express their first preference for a party that they would not have chosen using the simple plurality system. The second reason, linked to the first, is that there are different types of proportional system and they would each give slightly different results. Some systems are more proportional than others.

In this sense it is important to point out that it is simply not accurate to talk about proportionality as if it were some absolute. The systems which will be examined in this chapter are not equally proportional. This is largely to do with the exact manner in which the systems operate, the size of the constituencies and other such factors. The systems may not even display the same degrees of proportionality over time, as socio-political forces change absolute and relative voting preferences.

This chapter cannot provide any accurate guide to a future where the House of Commons is elected by a proportional electoral system; that, as has been seen, depends upon the voters. Since 1997, however, a number of proportional systems have been introduced for certain elections in the United Kingdom. For the first time we can see the impact of these systems without having to look to other countries for evidence.

There are hundreds of voting systems in operation around the world and it would be a pointless exercise in a book of this nature to offer an exhaustive account of them all. Indeed, it is often the case that these systems are variations on a particular theme. What follows therefore are examples of three systems that are all used in UK elections, each illustrating the main themes characterising most of the voting systems used in free, democratic countries. The three systems will be examined in three separate sections of this chapter: the party list system; the single transferable vote; and the additional member system.

The party list system

This type of system is in widespread use in countries across Europe. There are a number of types of list system and these became established along with the widening of adult suffrage in the late nineteenth and early twentieth centuries. Many of these systems emerged as it became clear that although majoritarian systems ensured that individual MPs were elected with a majority of the vote in a given constituency, they did not necessarily prevent a disproportionate result on a national level.

In many ways the party list is the most straightforward voting system of all those outlined in this book; however, the workings of these systems can be very complex and it will not be possible to examine these in detail here.

The system explained
Instead of voting for a named candidate, voters receive a ballot paper with the names of the political parties. This is the only system outlined in this book where voters do not have the name of a person to vote for. Depending on the variant of this system, the whole country is either classed as one massive constituency or is broken down into a number of large regional voting areas, each returning a number of representatives. This would be more accurately termed the regional party list system.

In its simplest form, the votes are added up and the final percentages calculated for each party. If Labour achieved 40 per cent of the vote and there are 646 seats in the House of Commons, it would be awarded 258 seats. The party would have produced a list of candidates and in this case the top 258 names on the list would be elected. This system is somewhat novel, as it removes any power that the voter might have in choosing one candidate in preference to another. In Britain, critics of the simple plurality system note that one of its major weaknesses is the lack of voter input into candidate selection. The list system would appear to take this notion to its logical conclusion in that the ballot paper contains no candidate names at all. This system is also known as the closed list system.

Variation – the open list

The closed list system, with a list of names published by each party, is effectively a fait accompli. Voters have no power to determine who is on the list. Some countries, however, operate a system using an open list. In such cases, as well as receiving a ballot paper offering a choice of political parties, voters also receive a list of candidates for each of the parties standing in the election. They then have the opportunity of choosing their preferred candidate from the list of their chosen party.

The list system has many other variations on the theme. It is probably the most proportional of all systems, since, as mentioned above, the country may be classed as one big constituency, then a very close match may be made between the number of votes cast and the number of seats obtained. This is particularly important for minor political parties who find that smaller constituencies are normally afforded few opportunities to build up sufficiently large numbers of votes to enable them to gain representation in a national assembly (this is a particular problem of the simple plurality system). The concept of **district magnitude** needs to be considered at this point. This relates to the fact that as the size of constituency and the number of representatives in the constituency increase, so does the proportionality of the system. A political system made up of one big constituency with, for example, 650 representatives elected by a single list would have an exceptionally high level of proportionality. Conversely, the simple plurality system in the UK has 650 constituencies, each returning a single representative, which means a low level of proportionality.

It will be useful to examine the workings of the list system in a real-life situation. Two case studies are presented below. The first analyses a country where there is just one single list. In the second there is an examination of the operation of a regional list system.

Box 4.1 Case study: elections in Israel

The Israeli electoral system has been the subject of much debate in recent years. Many have argued that the system is a contributory factor to the delicate political and security situation that exists in the Middle East.

Israel operates a list system based upon the country being one large constituency with each political party producing a single nationwide list. Given that Israel has a land area only slightly larger than Wales and a population of 7.3 million, slightly less than the population of London, this arrangement may make a lot more sense than in the UK as a whole, with nearly 61 million inhabitants and a land area twelve times as large as Israel's.

The Israeli Parliament, the **Knesset**, has 120 members elected by party list. The main political parties in the country draw up lists of candidates. There is no set way in which the lists are drawn but the Kadima, Labor and Likud parties all compile their lists through primary elections among registered party members. In some of the ultra-religious parties, their spiritual leaders appoint the candidates on their lists.

An electoral formula (the **D'Hondt Formula**) is used to deal with the issue of **remaindered votes**. There is never going to be a perfect match between the percentage of votes and the seats achieved by a party. It is likely that a party will obtain more than enough votes for say fifty seats, but not enough for fifty-one, and thus the excess (or remaindered) votes over those needed for fifty seats need to be redistributed.

Since 2003, a quota of 2 per cent of the national vote must be achieved (it was previously 1.5 per cent) before a political party can get any representation in the Knesset. This means that a number of parties might get no seats at all, but between them they may achieve more than 2 per cent of the vote. Two lists can reach an agreement regarding the distribution of excess votes between them before the elections. A device exists in this and a number of other list-based systems to enable smaller political parties to link their lists together and hence benefit from jointly achieving a vote above the threshold. This is called **apparentement** and requires prior formal agreement between the parties concerned.

The most recent general election in Israel was in 2009 in the aftermath of the crisis in Gaza. The main political parties were Kadima, led by Tzipi Livni, Labor, led by Ehud Barak, and the Likud Party, led by Benjamin Netanyahu. There was also the rising Yisrael Beiteinu

Party and its leader, Avigdor Lieberman. The following table offers a summary of the results of the 2009 general election in Israel.

The result suggests a narrow victory for the Kadima party, as it has the greatest percentage of votes and thus wins the largest number of seats. However, there was no overall majority (Kadima obtained just under a quarter of the seats). Once all the minor parties had pledged their support to the larger ones, it emerged that Likud would form a coalition with Lieberman's Yisrael Beiteinu Party, which, with a number of smaller right-wing parties, were willing to sustain Netanyahu in office as the new Prime Minister of Israel.

Table 4.2 The 2009 general election to the Israeli Knesset

Name of list	No. of valid votes	% of total votes	No. of seats
Kadima	758,032	22.5	28
Likud	729,054	21.6	27
Yisrael Beitenu	394,577	11.7	15
Labor	334,900	9.9	13
Shas	286,300	8.5	11
United Torah Judaism	147,954	4.4	5
Ra'am-Ta'al	113,954	3.4	4
Ichud Leumi	112,570	3.3	4
Hadash	112,130	3.3	4
New Movement – Meretz	99,611	3.0	3
Habayit Hayehudi	96,765	2.9	3
National Democratic Assembly – Balad	83,739	2.5	3

No. of eligible voters: 5,278,985

Valid votes: 3,373,490

Qualifying threshold (2%): 67,470

Votes per seat: 27,246

Source: The Knesset.

Box 4.2 Case study: UK elections to the European Parliament

After the Labour Party's victory in the 1997 general election, the Blair government introduced changes into the way that the United Kingdom's Members of the European Parliament are elected. Since the first elections in 1979, MEPs had been elected using the simple plurality system in relatively large single-member constituencies. The new system uses the closed, regional party list.

Currently the United Kingdom elects seventy-two MEPs to the European Parliament. The UK is divided into twelve regions, each of which is represented by between three and ten MEPs, depending on the size of the electorate.

This comprises nine regions in England, each returning a given number of MEPs. The smallest, England North-East, returns three MEPs and the largest, South East England, returns ten. London returns eight and Scotland, Wales and Northern Ireland are each classed as a single region returning six, four and three respectively. Each political party produces a list of candidates for each of the regions for which they are contesting the elections.

Most political parties will compete in nearly all the regions. Those parties with a specific regional or nationalist appeal will normally choose to contest the election only in the area where their cause will have some resonance with the electorate. The Scottish National Party, for example, only contests those seats available in Scotland. Likewise, Plaid Cymru, the Welsh nationalists, restrict their campaign to the Welsh 'region'.

The ballot paper in European elections now contains the names of the all the political parties fighting in the region as well as the names of any independent candidates that may be standing in the area. Below is a section of a ballot paper used in the South East region in the first European Parliamentary elections to use the party list system in 2009. (The actual ballot paper itself is longer, with a total of fifteen political parties appearing on it.)

As with the list system used in Israel, the number of MEP seats each party wins is directly proportional to the number of votes cast for them in each region. Clearly, the result in a regional list-based system will be less proportional than in a system such as Israel's where there is only one large constituency with a single list for each political party. The concept of district magnitude applies here: the larger the constituency and the greater the number of representatives in that constituency, the more proportional the result of the election will be.

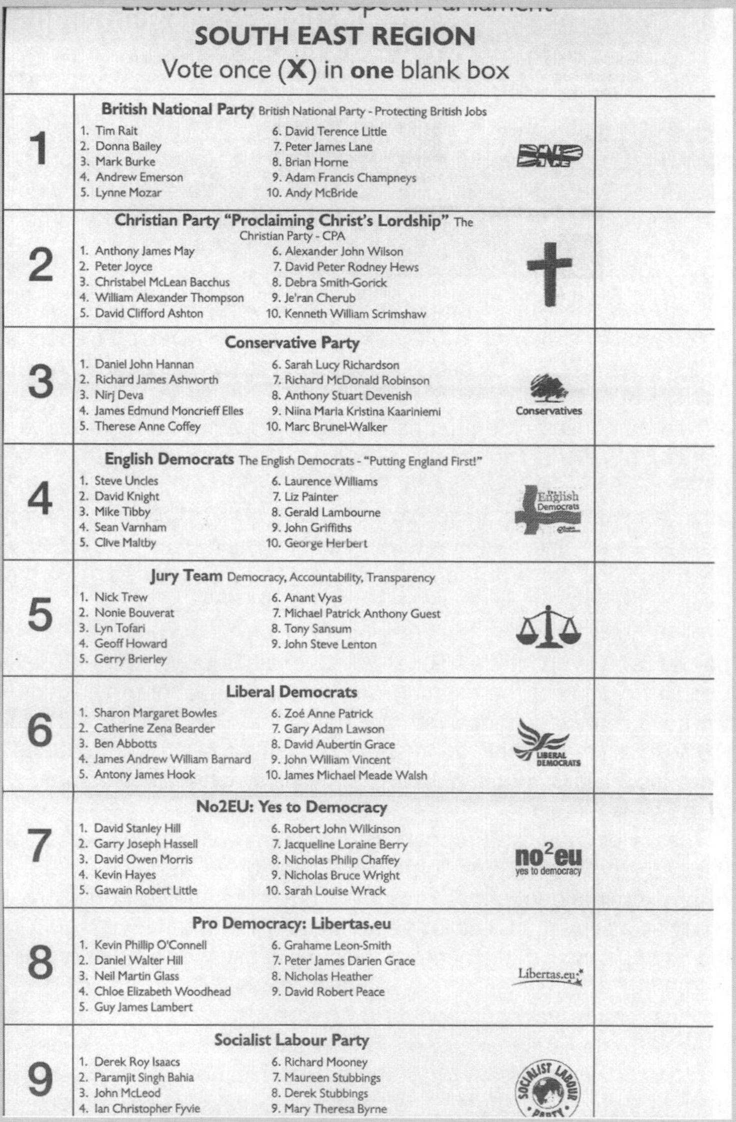

SOUTH EAST REGION

Vote once (**X**) in **one** blank box

1   **British National Party** British National Party - Protecting British Jobs

1. Tim Rait
2. Donna Bailey
3. Mark Burke
4. Andrew Emerson
5. Lynne Mozar
6. David Terence Little
7. Peter James Lane
8. Brian Horne
9. Adam Francis Champneys
10. Andy McBride

2   **Christian Party "Proclaiming Christ's Lordship"** The Christian Party - CPA

1. Anthony James May
2. Peter Joyce
3. Christabel McLean Bacchus
4. William Alexander Thompson
5. David Clifford Ashton
6. Alexander John Wilson
7. David Peter Rodney Hews
8. Debra Smith-Gorick
9. Je'ran Cherub
10. Kenneth William Scrimshaw

3   **Conservative Party**

1. Daniel John Hannan
2. Richard James Ashworth
3. Nirj Deva
4. James Edmund Moncrieff Elles
5. Therese Anne Coffey
6. Sarah Lucy Richardson
7. Richard McDonald Robinson
8. Anthony Stuart Devenish
9. Niina Maria Kristina Kaariniemi
10. Marc Brunel-Walker

Conservatives

4   **English Democrats** The English Democrats - "Putting England First!"

1. Steve Uncles
2. David Knight
3. Mike Tibby
4. Sean Varnham
5. Clive Maltby
6. Laurence Williams
7. Liz Painter
8. Gerald Lambourne
9. John Griffiths
10. George Herbert

English Democrats

5   **Jury Team** Democracy, Accountability, Transparency

1. Nick Trew
2. Nonie Bouverat
3. Lyn Tofari
4. Geoff Howard
5. Gerry Brierley
6. Anant Vyas
7. Michael Patrick Anthony Guest
8. Tony Sansum
9. John Steve Lenton

6   **Liberal Democrats**

1. Sharon Margaret Bowles
2. Catherine Zena Bearder
3. Ben Abbotts
4. James Andrew William Barnard
5. Antony James Hook
6. Zoé Anne Patrick
7. Gary Adam Lawson
8. David Aubertin Grace
9. John William Vincent
10. James Michael Meade Walsh

LIBERAL DEMOCRATS

7   **No2EU: Yes to Democracy**

1. David Stanley Hill
2. Garry Joseph Hassell
3. David Owen Morris
4. Kevin Hayes
5. Gawain Robert Little
6. Robert John Wilkinson
7. Jacqueline Loraine Berry
8. Nicholas Philip Chaffey
9. Nicholas Bruce Wright
10. Sarah Louise Wrack

no²eu
yes to democracy

8   **Pro Democracy: Libertas.eu**

1. Kevin Phillip O'Connell
2. Daniel Walter Hill
3. Neil Martin Glass
4. Chloe Elizabeth Woodhead
5. Guy James Lambert
6. Grahame Leon-Smith
7. Peter James Darien Grace
8. Nicholas Heather
9. David Robert Peace

Libertas.eu

9   **Socialist Labour Party**

1. Derek Roy Isaacs
2. Paramjit Singh Bahia
3. John McLeod
4. Ian Christopher Fyvie
6. Richard Mooney
7. Maureen Stubbings
8. Derek Stubbings
9. Mary Theresa Byrne

SOCIALIST LABOUR PARTY

Figure 4.1 Ballot paper from European Parliamentary elections

Compare Israel, with 120 representatives in one constituency, with the UK regional list system, where there are 72 representatives divided among 12 regions. The Israeli electoral system has a higher level of proportionality built into it.

Figure 4.2 and Table 4.3 illustrate the regional and party results for the most recent European Parliamentary elections in 2009.

As can be seen from the table and figure, the Conservatives and Labour received more than half the seats between them (thirty-eight out of seventy-two). However, this represents a much smaller combined share of the seats (53 per cent) than they achieved in the House of Commons after the 2005 general election (86 per cent). Indeed, up until the introduction of the closed regional party list for these elections in 1999, only Conservative and Labour Party candidates had ever won seats in the European Parliament. In the 1989 elections to the European Parliament, the Greens polled 15 per cent nationally and yet failed to win a single seat. The reason for this was undoubtedly the workings of the simple plurality system in which nothing is gained by amassing large numbers of votes across the country, but all that matters is gaining the largest number of votes within a single constituency boundary.

Since 1999, the position has been different. In 1999 and 2004, both the Greens and the United Kingdom Independence Party (UKIP) won seats in European Parliamentary elections. Indeed, as may be seen in the above figure, UKIP scored the same number of seats as the Labour Party, pushing the Liberals into fourth place (UKIP actually beat Labour into third place if one looks at votes rather than seats).

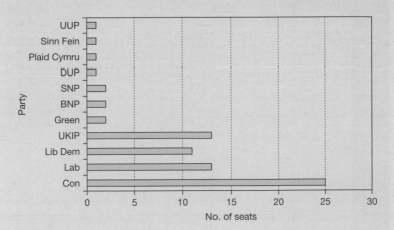

Figure 4.2 Results of the UK elections to the European Parliament 2009 (by party)

Table 4.3 Results of the UK elections to the European Parliament 2009 (by region)

	Con	Lab	Lib Dems	UKIP	Green	BNP	SNP	DUP	Plaid Cymru	Sinn Fein	UUP	Regional Total
Northern Ireland	0	0	0	0	0	0	0	1	0	1	1	3
Scotland	1	2	1	0	0	0	2	0	0	0	0	6
Wales	1	1	0	1	0	0	0	0	1	0	0	4
London	3	2	1	1	1	0	0	0	0	0	0	8
East Midlands	2	1	1	1	0	0	0	0	0	0	0	5
Eastern	3	1	1	2	0	0	0	0	0	0	0	7
North East	1	1	1	0	0	0	0	0	0	0	0	3
North West	3	2	1	1	0	1	0	0	0	0	0	8
South East	4	1	2	2	1	0	0	0	0	0	0	10
South West	3	0	1	2	0	0	0	0	0	0	0	6
West Midlands	2	1	1	2	0	0	0	0	0	0	0	6
Yorkshire & The Humber	2	1	1	1	0	1	0	0	0	0	0	6
Total seats	25	13	11	13	2	2	2	1	1	1	1	72

Implications for governance and representation

Today, most countries operate the regional variant of the party list system. Regional list systems enable local lists to be published by the political parties, the aim of which is to provide greater contact between voters and their elected representatives. It remains the case, however, that list-based systems do not provide for the individual constituency-based MP. As such, the nature of representation in countries with list-based systems is significantly affected.

The simplicity of the system outlined above is somewhat complicated by a variety of methods by which the counting of votes may take place. A number of quotas have been devised to ensure the fair representation of smaller political parties. Again there is no space in this book to describe these formulae, but for a fuller discussion on the variety of quotas that may be employed for use with list systems, see David Farrell, who offers a sensible round-up.[1]

As voters are not electing representatives as candidates, but from lists provided by the political parties, the question of who wins in these elections should really be the question of which party wins. The successful individuals will probably owe their success to their loyalty and hard work for their party and not to any trust and respect which may have been built up with the local electorate. In this respect it may be seen that the list-based system is likely to concentrate even more power in the hands of the political parties and this is why some adherents of proportional representation do not favour this system.

The whole nature of constituency representation is also called into question in list systems. This is possibly one of the reasons why the list-based system has little support among even pro-reform politicians in Britain when considering replacing the simple plurality system for UK parliamentary elections. The very idea of abandoning constituency representation, which to many observers is the very cornerstone of the UK democratic system, would be unthinkable.

The result of an election run on the lines of a list system is likely to be very proportional. This will especially be the case if the country is treated as one large constituency, as happens in Israel (see the case study). The likelihood of this happening in Britain is also very remote given the regional variations in voting behaviour that are apparent. Scotland and Wales have additional parties (such as the SNP and Plaid Cymru), and in Northern Ireland, the party system is completely different from in Great Britain. Some form of sub-national or region-based list would be one solution to the problem.

As mentioned above, one of the problems of decreasing the size of the district will be that this reduces the proportionality of the system. One way in which the effects of this may be mitigated is by having a two-tier system of districts. In such a system the inefficiencies and waste caused at the lower tier are compensated for at the higher tier. In practice this means that parties who might be penalised because of the regional nature of the list (the Greens, for example, who might not poll sufficient votes in one district to get elected, might obtain representation when all the wasted votes from all the districts are collected at the higher tier).

Such a system would provide small parties with very little support in any one area with the opportunity to gain seats in an elected assembly. However, there is the danger that a small party such as this would, in a finely balanced Parliament, be able to wield influence far out of proportion to its true level of support. For this reason, most countries using a list-based system operate some level of **voting threshold**, above which a party must poll before gaining any seats in an assembly.

The list system is probably the closest there is to pure proportional representation. As we have seen in detail, however, this does rather depend on the quota system used in the counting process, a vote threshold and variation between single national lists and multiple regional lists. A certain measure of disproportionality may still occur. The system is clearly attractive; the many countries using one or other variation of the list is a very clear indication of this.

In spite of the attractiveness of the system, which makes it by far the most popular voting system in Europe, and despite the fact that it has been introduced for UK elections to the European Parliament, it does not necessarily follow that such a system would be attractive in the United Kingdom for elections to the House of Commons. Few politicians, academics and journalists could conceive of reforming the United Kingdom constitution in such a manner that would effectively sever the bond that has long since connected Members of Parliament with their constituents.

The Labour government's decision to adopt a variant of the list system should not be interpreted as a commitment to anything more than the desire to change the way that UK MEPs are elected. No doubt part of the thinking behind this particular decision was to move away from the situation where out of all the MEPs in Brussels and Strasbourg, only those from the UK were elected using a non-proportional electoral system.

The single transferable vote

One of the main criticisms of the party list system is its failure to provide adequate constituency-based representation. It may be argued that this weakens the bond that exists between voters and their elected representatives. The single transferable vote (STV) is an electoral system which overcomes this difficulty. STV combines proportionality with constituency-based representation. One of the main differences between STV and the simple plurality system, supplementary vote, second ballot and Alternative Vote also concerns constituencies. Whereas these latter systems are based on single-member constituencies, the single transferable vote uses multi-member constituencies.

The concept of district magnitude once again needs to be considered. It would not be possible to provide proportionality in a system solely reliant on representatives elected in single-member constituencies. The district must be large enough and a number of representatives need to be returned within that district, involving some form of vote redistribution to enable the result to be proportional. When discussing the list system, it was seen that if the regions are too big then it is difficult to establish an effective link between representative and constituent. The single transferable vote represents something of a compromise in this respect.

This system is not widely used. Eire (the Republic of Ireland) uses it for legislative elections. It is also the preferred voting system of the Liberal Democrats and the Electoral Reform Society. Perhaps more significantly, it is actually a system which has been used for a number of years in all local and European elections in Northern Ireland. After the referendum which endorsed the **Good Friday Agreement**, the new Northern Ireland Assembly was established and it was decided that the single transferable vote would be used as the system for electing its members.

The system explained

As with the supplementary vote, voting in the single transferable vote is preferential. STV is more like the alternative vote, however, because electors are not restricted in the number of preferences that they may express. Voters express preferences for candidates (1, 2, 3, 4 and so on). The aim of the system is more ambitious, however. Instead of simply ensuring that a candidate is elected with over half of the vote (the point of majoritarian systems such as the supplementary vote), the aim is to achieve proportionality, in other words to ensure that the number of seats gained by a political party is in proportion to the percentage of votes that it receives. The workings of preferential majoritarian systems are also similar up to a point; both involve the redistribution of votes according to the second preferences on ballot papers. In STV, however, candidates do not have to obtain 50 per cent plus one vote to be elected. Clearly, that would make no sense in a constituency electing more than one MP.

The number of votes required for a candidate to get elected varies from constituency to constituency, depending on the size of the total vote and the number of representatives to be returned. This number is expressed in the form of a formula or quota. The following formula (the **Droop Quota**) determines the number of votes that are needed to win a seat in a constituency.

$$\frac{\text{Number of Votes Cast}}{\text{Number of Seats} + 1} + 1$$

If, in a constituency, 100,000 votes are cast and there are four seats to be won, then the above formula would be translated as follows:

$$\frac{100,000}{5} + 1 = 20,001$$

In this constituency a candidate must achieve 20,001 votes to get elected. If no candidate on the ballot paper achieves this figure then, just as with the alternative vote, the candidate with the fewest number of first-preference votes is eliminated from the count and his or her votes are redistributed among the other candidates on the basis of the second preferences expressed.

In all likelihood, however, one candidate probably will reach the quota in the first round of counting; indeed, it is probable that a candidate will obtain more than the necessary quota of first preferences, perhaps 25,000 in the case of the hypothetical constituency above. One of the main reasons why the simple plurality system is not proportional is because smaller parties may obtain hundreds of thousands of votes nationally, but insufficient numbers at constituency level to win any seats. This problem is compounded by successful candidates winning seats with large majorities of votes, far in excess of any requirement to win.

The single transferable vote aims to deal with both these issues. Candidates cannot hold on to any votes beyond the quota needed to win a seat in the constituency. Once a candidate has reached the required quota to be elected, any votes in excess of this figure are redistributed to other candidates, again according to the second preferences. In the above example, it was suggested that a candidate might obtain 25,000 first preferences (in other words 4,999 more than the quota requires). In this case the 4,999 'excess' votes are redistributed to the other candidates.

There immediately arises a problem from the redistribution of the votes that are in excess of the quota. When redistributing the votes of an eliminated candidate, all the votes are redistributed to the other candidates who have been ranked in second place on the eliminated candidate's first-preference ballot papers. When redistributing the excess votes of an elected candidate there is the question of which votes are to be redistributed. Remember in the example given above, only 4,999 of the 25,000 votes are to be redistributed. Which 4,999?

In order to answer the question, one must try to see what the point of this system is. Clearly, any redistribution of second-preference votes should reflect the spread of opinions of those electors whose votes are being allocated. If half of the voters who chose candidate A gave a second preference to candidate C, it seems only fair that half of the redistributed excess votes are transferred from candidate A to candidate C. Once an accurate idea is gained of how all of the second preferences were expressed it is possible to assign a weighting to each vote cast. In the above example, therefore, all 25,000 votes are looked at and reallocated as fractions. If half of the 25,000 nominate just one other candidate in second preference then half of the excess votes are allocated to that candidate (half of 4,999 equals 2,499 votes). This is really the only fair way to reallocate the votes.

Whole votes are reallocated from those candidates eliminated from the count (if a candidate fails to reach the quota) and fractions of votes (adding up to the excess votes) are reallocated from those candidates who obtain more than the quota of votes. Many students have difficulty with this process of reallocation at the 'top and tail' of the ballot, and the complexity of the counting process has led some to believe that the system as a whole is unduly complicated. While it is clear that the counting process is complex, voters should find the system no more difficult to understand than the Alternative Vote. The key difference here is in the number of candidates from each party which appear on the ballot paper. Ballot papers are therefore likely to be long.

In a constituency which returns four representatives, it is likely that a number of political parties will each put up four candidates and thus that candidates from the same party will be competing with each other as well as with the opposing parties' candidates for the first preferences of the voters. This means that a Labour voter faced with four Labour candidates must choose one to award the first preference. The others would presumably appear second, third and fourth on the voter's ballot paper. It could be, however, that one of the Labour candidates is not popular with the voter, in which case the candidate might be placed after a Liberal Democrat candidate or even omitted altogether.

Proponents of this system believe it is the only one that offers voters a real say in the election of candidates. Instead of being presented with a fait accompli by the political parties (that is, one candidate), voters will be able to choose not only between political parties, but between candidates from the same political party. Against it could be argued that instead of a fait accompli of one candidate, voters will be presented with a fait accompli of four or five. After all, the candidates will all have been selected by the party and the choice is preordained by the party leadership and a continuation of the same centralisation that exists in modern political life.

Box 4.3 Case study: elections to the Northern Ireland Assembly

The Northern Ireland Assembly was established under the terms of the Belfast Agreement (also known as the Good Friday Agreement) and was first elected in June 1998. The eighteen Westminster parliamentary constituencies are used for the Assembly elections (see map below). Six seats are allocated to each constituency, giving a total of one hundred and eight seats. The geographical boundaries for the eighteen constituencies have remained unchanged since the first Assembly election in 1998. These are indicated by the map below.

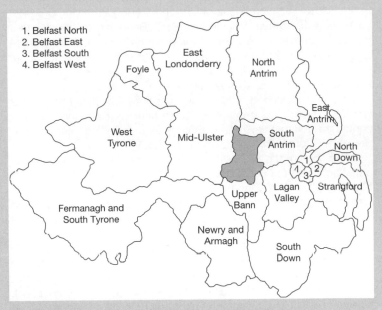

1. Belfast North
2. Belfast East
3. Belfast South
4. Belfast West

Foyle

East Londonderry

North Antrim

East Antrim

West Tyrone

Mid-Ulster

South Antrim

North Down

Fermanagh and South Tyrone

Upper Bann

Lagan Valley

Strangford

Newry and Armagh

South Down

Figure 4.3 Northern Ireland parliamentary constituencies

Voters use the preferential system of voting. By casting a vote 1, 2, 3 and so on, the voter is telling the returning officer, '(1) A is my preferred choice, but if A does not need my vote or has no chance of being elected, (2) transfer my vote to B; if B does not need my vote and has no chance of being elected, (3) transfer my vote to C and so on.'

The formula to establish the quota is that outlined above. This quota is properly known as the Droop Quota (see above).

The system is a complex one, although the voters in Northern Ireland are used to this system as it has been used in local elections for many years. The electorate there seem to have developed an instinctive feeling about how to transfer their votes. It must also be said that the counting process is very time-consuming. Indeed, it is usually the evening of the following day before there is some idea of what the new Assembly will look like.

The most recent elections to the Northern Ireland Assembly were in February 2007. Table 4.4 shows the results in one of the eighteen multi-member constituencies.

In the case of the South Down constituency, no candidate achieved the 6,588 first-preference votes required to secure a seat. In the first reallocation, Malachi Curran (Labour), receiving only 123 votes, was eliminated, followed by Peter Bowles (Conservative) for the second reallocation. If one looks at the column on the far right of the table, it may be seen that it was not until the seventh count that the first of the candidates achieved the quota and not until the eleventh count that all six seats were filled.

It is worth looking at another of the eighteen results of the 2007 Northern Ireland Assembly election to see what happens when a candidate does achieve the quota required to win a seat on first-preference votes. This is shown in Table 4.5.

In the case of the Mid-Ulster constituency, four of the six candidates achieved the quota of 6,326 on the first count. In the case of Martin McGuinness (Sinn Féin), 1,739 votes in excess of the quota were distributed to other candidates. As it happened, the other Sinn Féin candidates, Francis Molloy and Michelle O'Neill, did not require these excess votes because they too were elected with the quota of first-preference votes. It is quite possible that Patsy McGlone (SDLP) did benefit from some of the votes of Kathleen Lagan (SDLP), who was the sixth candidate to be eliminated from the count. Similarly, William Armstrong (UUP), the last of the six candidates to win a seat, was probably helped by some of the other unionist candidates eliminated from the contest and perhaps even Ian McCrea (DUP), some of whose excess votes might eventually have made a contribution to the election of the sixth representative.

Table 4.6 illustrates the distribution of seats for all parties in the March 2007 Northern Ireland Assembly results.

The Belfast Agreement was not simply about restoring a devolved assembly to Northern Ireland. In addition, it made provision for a Northern Ireland government, based on the principle of power sharing. Between the 1960s and the 1990s, Northern Ireland was

Table 4.4 The 2007 Northern Ireland Assembly election (South Down)

Candidate (Party)	No. of first-preference votes	% of votes	Elected on count
Caitriona Ruane (SF)	6,334	13.74	7th count
Margaret Ritchie (SDLP)	5,838	12.66	8th count
P. J. Bradley (SDLP)	5,652	12.26	9th count
Jim Wells (DUP)	5,542	12.02	10th count
William Clark (SF)	5,138	11.14	8th count
John McCallister (UUP)	4,447	9.64	11th count
Michael Carr (SDLP)	2,972	6.45	
Eamonn McConvey (SF)	2,662	5.77	
William Burns (DUP)	2,611	5.66	
Ciaran Mussen (GP)	1,622	3.52	
Henry Reilly (UKIP)	1,229	2.67	
David Griffin (APNI)	691	1.50	
Martin Cunningham (Ind) [Ind Rep]	434	0.94	
Frederick Wharton (UKUP)	424	0.92	
Peter Bowles (Con)	391	0.85	
Malachi Curran Labour (Lab)	123	0.27	
Total	46,110	100.00	

Electorate: 71,704

Turnout: 46,623

Total Valid Poll: 46,110

Quota: 6,588

Table 4.5 The 2007 Northern Ireland Assembly election (Mid-Ulster)

Candidate (Party)	No. of first-preference votes	% of votes	Elected on count
Martin McGuinness (SF)	8,065	18.21	1st count
Ian McCrea (DUP)	7,608	17.18	1st count
Francis Molloy (SF)	6,597	14.90	1st count
Michelle O'Neill (SF)	6,432	14.53	1st count
Patsy McGlone (SDLP)	4,976	11.24	5th count
William Armstrong (UUP)	4,781	10.80	7th count
Kathleen Lagan (SDLP)	2,759	6.23	
Walter Millar (UKUP)	1,210	2.73	
Elizabeth Forde (DUP)	1,021	2.31	
Brendan McLaughlin (Ind) [RSF]	437	0.99	
Margaret Marshall (APNI)	221	0.50	
Harry Hutchinson (Ind)	170	0.38	
Total	44,277	100.00	

Electorate: 61,223

Turnout: 44,728

Total Valid Poll: 44,277

Quota: 6,326

a very seriously divided place. These divisions were both religious (Catholic versus Protestant) and political (unionist versus nationalist). The idea of power sharing was to bring together figures from both the unionist/Protestant and nationalist/Catholic communities. The Belfast Agreement provided for the political parties with the greatest and second-greatest number of seats to form a power-sharing government. In 2007, the Democratic Unionist Party and Sinn Féin came in first and second place and former arch-enemies Ian Paisley

Table 4.6 The 2007 Northern Ireland Assembly election

Party	No. of seats
Democratic Unionist Party	36
Sinn Féin	28
Ulster Unionist Party	18
Social Democratic and Labour Party	16
Alliance	7
Green Party	1
Independent Health Coalition	1
Progressive Unionist Party	1

and Martin McGuinness became the First Minister and Deputy First Minister of Northern Ireland.

Another reason for adopting the single transferable vote for elections to the Northern Ireland Assembly was to attempt to overcome one-party dominance in a single-member constituency. In a divided community such as Northern Ireland, a multi-member constituency provides the opportunity for representatives from more than one of the political and religious traditions to be elected, thus providing greater confidence in the political system on the part of the voters. Following the 2007 elections, fourteen of the eighteen constituencies have representatives of the unionist/Protestant and nationalist/Catholic communities. Three are dominated by unionists, but also contain non-aligned Alliance representatives. Only one constituency, West Belfast, is wholly represented by members of one (in this case, the nationalist) community. In this sense, therefore, one of the main aims of using STV has been achieved.

Implications for governance and representation

This system is already used for some elections in the United Kingdom. The peculiarly divided nature of life in Northern Ireland may have led to its introduction there. Interestingly, there was no suggestion that this system should be introduced for election to the other devolved bodies in Scotland and Wales (although it has been introduced for local elections in Scotland). It is a doubtful prospect that such a system will gain wider support and replace the simple plurality system for elections to the House of Commons.

The single transferable vote does overcome one of the major concerns expressed about the list system in that the link between the voter and the MP is maintained, whilst at the same time providing a proportional result. In order to achieve this, however, the size of constituencies would be necessarily large, perhaps with between two and three hundred thousand inhabitants; this would make the job of representation very difficult, especially in very sparsely populated regions such as the Highlands and Islands of Scotland (where the Westminster constituencies are already geographically massive). Furthermore, some constituencies might lack coherence once one has moved out of the urban centres. In addition, the nature of constituency representation with this system would not be the same as exists in Britain at present. The link would be broken between the constituency and the individual MP.

The system is not as proportional as other systems. This is mainly due to the fact that, in breaking the country down into unlinked constituencies, some compromise of proportionality has had to be made (the notion of district magnitude suggests that the larger the constituency, the more proportional the result).

The system would undoubtedly provide greater flexibility for the voter who could rank candidates within and between parties in order of preference. Constituents would be able to choose from perhaps five MPs when seeking help for a particular problem, meaning that voters would be able to express their political views more effectively. In preferring one candidate within a party rather than another, the voter would be showing support for one wing or body of opinion within the party. It is probable that within any constituency there could be MPs from two or three political parties.

Conversely, it may be argued that voters would simply maintain their tribal loyalties and restrict their choices to a single party. There is evidence, however, to suggest that this may not be the case. Dunleavy, Margetts and Weir provide survey data which suggested half of all respondents were willing to express preferences for candidates of more than one party.[2]

It is unlikely that the political parties would be happy to lose control in elections and perhaps the introduction of STV would lead to even more strenuous efforts to ensure candidate selection was still in the hands of the party machine. In recent years, the increasing tendency towards centralisation (particularly within the Labour and Conservative parties) has been likely to ensure a greater uniformity of candidate, loyal and 'on message'.

A political party would need to attract the support of over 50 per cent of the national vote to form a government. If this did not happen, the most likely outcome would be a coalition government and supporters of the system argue that this would provide sensible, consensual politics, rather than the adversarial dogfight which has typified the British political system hitherto. Critics of coalition governments argue that this would create instability and weakness. Although there are times when consensus and agreement is necessary, there are also times when boldness and resolution are required in politics and the chances of getting this through coalition are remote.

It may be argued that the system overall is too complicated and that it is insufficiently transparent for voters to trust. In response to this, however, it must be said that the electorate in Northern Ireland as well as voters in the Irish Republic, which also uses it for elections to the **Dáil** (the Irish Parliament), appear to be very comfortable with the single transferable vote. Of course, the argument that if it works in one country then it will work in another is not necessarily a valid one. However, there have been numerous surveys in which voters have been subject to 'mock-elections' run on STV rules, and respondents seem to have had few problems with the system.

Perhaps one of the most telling characteristics of the system is its lack of ubiquity. In short, there are very few countries that use it. Ireland uses it for parliamentary elections, as does Malta. In Australia it is used for elections to the Senate (upper House). There have been brief flirtations with it elsewhere but these have been short-lived. Political inertia might have been an excuse until twenty years ago, but since the growth of democracy in the former Soviet republics, one might have expected this system to have been adopted by at least some of these countries.

In fact, apart from a brief interlude in Estonia, no country has adopted the single transferable vote, which perhaps indicates that in spite of a spirited defence by the Liberal Democrats and the Electoral Reform Society in this country, it is not a favourite for adoption. Indeed, recent government proposals for elections to the Scottish Parliament and Welsh Assembly and to the European Parliament appear to have ruled STV out of the reckoning in favour of list-based systems.

The additional member system

This is a hybrid electoral system, in other words a combination of two of the previous voting systems already examined in this book. They are combined in a manner that produces a proportional result. The name of the system has been criticised and some would prefer to call it the 'two-vote system' because of the way in which this type of voting system has been adopted in some countries. Given that most people studying at this level will be familiar with the 'additional member' term, the system will be referred to in this way for the remainder of this book.

Perhaps the most prominent country to use this electoral system is Germany. One of the case studies later in the chapter offers an insight into the workings of the German system. The Scottish Parliament, the National Assembly for Wales and the Greater London Assembly also all use the additional member system to elect their representatives.

Like the single transferable vote, the additional member system seeks to combine proportionality with constituency representation and it is therefore often cited as a system which could be adopted in the UK without too much upheaval (see below). Unlike STV, it does not rely on preferential voting nor does it involve any complex counting procedure. Some would argue that it retains the best features of the simple plurality system whilst ensuring a high degree of proportionality.

The system explained
There are two key points which characterise this system: first, the voter has two votes to cast – these votes are cast at the same time – and second, two different 'types' of MP are elected to the assembly. The result will be an assembly made up of both constituency

representatives and a number of others, the additional members. It is the inclusion of this second group of representatives that makes this electoral system proportional.

Voters using this system cast one vote for a constituency MP. This process is identical to the simple plurality system in that when the counting of the votes takes place, the candidate with most votes will be elected, even if he or she polls fewer than half of the vote.

The second vote is cast for a party; the voter may vote for a party different from the one supported in the first vote. These votes are added up to give a national (or regional) total for each party. This second vote is list-based, in other words it is the parties themselves that determine which of their candidates are elected. It is the outcome of the second vote that will enable a proportional result to be achieved. The following hypothetical example may help illustrate how the system works.

In this example, the assembly to which representatives are being elected is composed of 100 MPs. The country is broken down into fifty constituencies. Each of these constituencies returns a single member, using the simple plurality system. The remaining fifty members are elected via the list system, according to the party share of the vote cast.

Table 4.7 shows the result involving four political parties in such a hypothetical election using the additional member voting system.

Effectively, the total number of seats achieved by a party will be based on the percentage of votes it receives through the list vote. This means that, as in the example above, some parties will have mostly constituency seats with a number of additional members, while other parties which have been unable to muster sufficient support in one constituency will receive most of, if not all, their seats from the list of additional members.

As may be seen from the above result, all the political parties benefit from the additional members but the system gives the greatest help to those smaller parties that fail to win any seats via the simple plurality vote. All the votes that these parties have achieved nationally deserve seats in the assembly.

This system may operate with a minimum threshold, above which a party must poll in order to gain representation. It may be argued that this is unfair, especially if, as in Germany, the threshold is set

Table 4.7 Hypothetical election result using AMS

Party	Constituency wins	% of party votes	Additional members	Total seats
Blue	25	40	15	40
Green	0	5	5	5
Orange	5	20	15	20
Red	20	35	15	35
Total	50	100	50	100

rather high (see below). On the other hand, it may be argued that if a threshold does not exist or is too low, then extremist parties might consequently be able to wield disproportionate influence.

Elections to the Welsh Assembly

The National Assembly for Wales is composed of sixty elected Members (AMs). For an Assembly election, which takes place every four years, each registered voter has two votes.

The first vote is for a local constituency Member. A Member is elected for each of the forty constituencies in Wales by the simple plurality system; the candidate with the greatest number of votes wins the seat.

The second vote is to elect a regional Member. Regional Members are elected using the party list electoral system. Each political party produces a list of candidates. Wales has five electoral regions, and four Members are elected from each region. The electoral regions are based on the European Parliamentary constituencies. Each electoral region covers between seven and nine constituencies. The electoral regions are:

- North Wales
- Mid and West Wales
- South Wales East
- South Wales West
- South Wales Central

Box 4.4 Case study: elections in Germany

The additional member system has been used in elections to the Bundestag since 1949, when self-government returned to Germany. Since then there have been thirteen general elections. Germany is often held up as a model by those who would like to see a proportional voting system used for elections to the House of Commons. For most of the post-war era, Germany has experienced great economic success combined with political stability. As such, it is an argument to confound critics of proportional representation who claim that it will lead to weak and unstable government.

As with the United Kingdom, the government of Germany derives from the governing party in the national assembly. The Bundestag is composed of 672 members who are returned using the dual system of election, outlined above. Half are directly elected, using the first-past-the-post system in the 336 constituencies, while the other half are elected indirectly by a list-based proportional system. The lists of candidates are drawn up by the political parties in each *Land* (state).

Below is part of a ballot paper used in a federal election in Germany. The paper is divided into two halves; the left-hand side contains the names of candidates hoping to win using the simple plurality system; the right-hand side contains the parties hoping to win seats using the list-based system.

The proportional result is the one that determines the overall number of seats that the party receives. In other words, a party receiving 40 per cent of the vote will gain sufficient 'additional members' to take the party to that percentage of seats (see figure above). It may be, however, that a party does so well in constituency seats in the state that they have a greater percentage of the seats than their vote entitles them to have. This is known as **overhang**, and parties in this situation cannot be denied any of these seats. Further, in Germany, the overall total of Bundestag seats must rise by the size of the overhang.

A threshold of 5 per cent exists for parties seeking representation via the list. If a party has won three constituency seats, however, then this threshold is not applicable. As with the list system of Israel, apparentement is possible, whereby smaller parties can formally link their lists so as to maximise their chances of gaining representation. The threshold has led to a sharp reduction in the number of parties being represented in the Bundestag, however. In 1949, there were twelve parties represented, but in the most recent general election, in 2009, there were only six parties with representatives in the Bundestag.

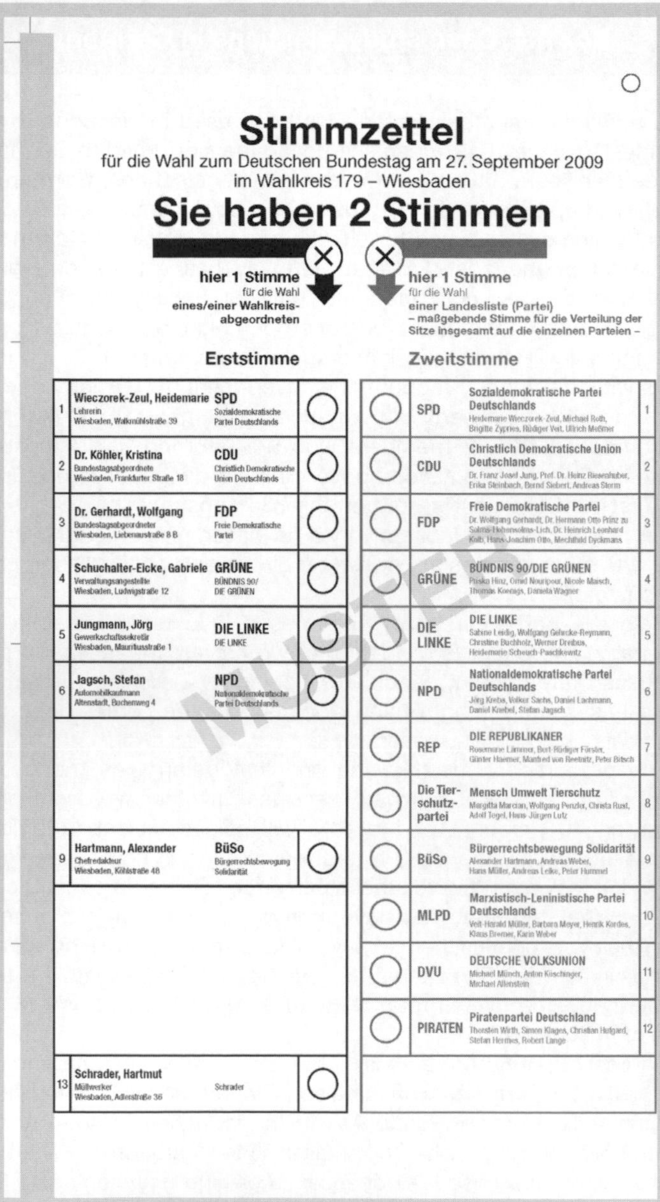

Stimmzettel

für die Wahl zum Deutschen Bundestag am 27. September 2009
im Wahlkreis 179 – Wiesbaden

Sie haben 2 Stimmen

hier 1 Stimme
für die Wahl
eines/einer Wahlkreis-abgeordneten

Erststimme

1	**Wieczorek-Zeul, Heidemarie** Lehrerin Wiesbaden, Walkmühlstraße 39	**SPD** Sozialdemokratische Partei Deutschlands	○
2	**Dr. Köhler, Kristina** Bundestagsabgeordnete Wiesbaden, Frankfurter Straße 18	**CDU** Christlich Demokratische Union Deutschlands	○
3	**Dr. Gerhardt, Wolfgang** Bundestagsabgeordneter Wiesbaden, Liebenaustraße 8 B	**FDP** Freie Demokratische Partei	○
4	**Schuchalter-Eicke, Gabriele** Verwaltungsangestellte Wiesbaden, Ludwigstraße 12	**GRÜNE** BÜNDNIS 90/ DIE GRÜNEN	○
5	**Jungmann, Jörg** Gewerkschaftssekretär Wiesbaden, Mauritiusstraße 1	**DIE LINKE** DIE LINKE	○
6	**Jagsch, Stefan** Automobilkaufmann Altenstadt, Buchenweg 4	**NPD** Nationaldemokratische Partei Deutschlands	○
9	**Hartmann, Alexander** Chefredakteur Wiesbaden, Köhlstraße 48	**BüSo** Bürgerrechtsbewegung Solidarität	○
13	**Schrader, Hartmut** Müllwerker Wiesbaden, Adlerstraße 36	Schrader	○

hier 1 Stimme
für die Wahl
einer Landesliste (Partei)
– maßgebende Stimme für die Verteilung der Sitze insgesamt auf die einzelnen Parteien –

Zweitstimme

○	**SPD**	**Sozialdemokratische Partei Deutschlands** Heidemarie Wieczorek-Zeul, Michael Roth, Brigitte Zypries, Rüdiger Veit, Ulrich Meßmer	1
○	**CDU**	**Christlich Demokratische Union Deutschlands** Dr. Franz Josef Jung, Prof. Dr. Heinz Riesenhuber, Erika Steinbach, Bernd Siebert, Andreas Storm	2
○	**FDP**	**Freie Demokratische Partei** Dr. Wolfgang Gerhardt, Dr. Hermann Otto Prinz zu Solms-Hohensolms-Lich, Dr. Heinrich Leonhard Kolb, Hans-Joachim Otto, Mechthild Dyckmans	3
○	**GRÜNE**	**BÜNDNIS 90/DIE GRÜNEN** Priska Hinz, Omid Nouripour, Nicole Maisch, Thomas Koenigs, Daniela Wagner	4
○	**DIE LINKE**	**DIE LINKE** Sabine Leidig, Wolfgang Gehrcke-Reymann, Christine Buchholz, Werner Dreibus, Heidemarie Scheuch-Paschkewitz	5
○	**NPD**	**Nationaldemokratische Partei Deutschlands** Jörg Krebs, Volker Sachs, Daniel Lachmann, Daniel Knebel, Stefan Jagsch	6
○	**REP**	**DIE REPUBLIKANER** Rosemarie Lämmer, Bert-Rüdiger Förster, Günter Haemer, Manfred von Reetnitz, Peter Bitsch	7
○	**Die Tierschutzpartei**	**Mensch Umwelt Tierschutz** Margitta Marcian, Wolfgang Penzler, Christa Rust, Adolf Tegel, Hans-Jürgen Lutz	8
○	**BüSo**	**Bürgerrechtsbewegung Solidarität** Alexander Hartmann, Andreas Weber, Hans Müller, Andreas Leike, Peter Hummel	9
○	**MLPD**	**Marxistisch-Leninistische Partei Deutschlands** Veit-Harald Müller, Barbara Meyer, Henrik Kordes, Klaus Bremer, Karin Weber	10
○	**DVU**	**DEUTSCHE VOLKSUNION** Michael Münch, Anton Köschinger, Michael Allenstein	11
○	**PIRATEN**	**Piratenpartei Deutschland** Thorsten Wirth, Simon Klages, Christian Hufgard, Stefan Hermes, Robert Lange	12

MUSTER

Figure 4.4 Ballot paper from federal election in Germany

Table 4.8 The 2005 German Bundestag election

Party	First votes	%	Direct seats	Second votes	%
Christian Democratic Union/Christian Social Union	19,280,940	40.9	150	16,631,049	35.2
Social Democratic Party of Germany (SPD)	18,129,100	38.4	145	16,194,665	34.2
Free Democratic Party (FDP)	2,208,531	4.7	0	4,648,144	9.8
The Left Party	3,764,168	8.0	3	4,118,194	8.7
Alliance 90/The Greens	2,538,913	5.4	1	3,838,326	8.1
National Democratic Party of Germany (NPD)	857,777	1.8	0	748,568	1.6
The Republicans	38,678	0.1	0	266,101	0.6
Others	375,955	0.8	0	842,941	1.8

Registered electors: 61,870,711

Voters: 48,044,134 (77.7%)

Valid first votes: 47,194,062 (98.2%)

Valid second votes: 47,287,988 (98.4%)

The result of the Bundestag election in September 2005 is represented in Table 4.8.

As may be seen from these results, there is not a perfect correlation between votes and seats (although this is almost impossible to achieve with any truly workable system). The main reason for this is because the proportional aspect of the system is based on each of the states which make up the Federal Republic of Germany. If the list becomes sub-national, then the problem of district magnitude once more needs to be considered: as the size of the area within which the election takes place decreases, so too does the proportionality of the result.

The German system has come in for some fierce criticism in recent years. This, frankly, has had more to do with the behaviour of the political parties than with the electoral system *per se*. Many argue that the voting system is instrumental in the problems which have been highlighted.

In 1980, the SPD (on the centre-left of the political spectrum) was in coalition with 'centre' party the FDP. In 1982, the FDP decided to walk out of the coalition and join the conservative CDU/CSU. The voters were not consulted, no election took place to determine the change of government that ensued and despite the FDP receiving no constituency **mandate**, it has managed to maintain a sufficient number of list seats in elections since then.

The FDP held court in Germany due to its strategic position between the parties of the left and right. It could be argued that in a system of proportional representation, this has been an almost irresistible position, enabling it to play the role of 'kingmaker' for many years. It is this factor which is perhaps worth considering when assessing the Liberal Democrats' advocacy of proportional representation.

Advocates of this system argue that it is not necessarily the centre party that holds sway. In the German federal elections in 1998 and 2001, it was the Greens that formed a junior coalition partnership with the SPD. Indeed, if one examines the outcome of the 2005 election, it may be seen that the SPD and the Greens were unable to form a coalition with a majority of seats. Furthermore, the Christian Democrats were unable to form a majority coalition with the FDP. The outcome was a so-called 'grand coalition' between the Christian Democrats and the Social Democrats. To put this into a UK context, it would be like the Conservative and Labour parties forming a government together. Critics of the system would argue that few, if any, German electors would have cast their votes for the two main political parties believing that they would be together in government.

The German political system has undergone tremendous upheaval after the unification of East and West and the resulting economic problems. It is tempting, therefore, to draw conclusions which blame Germany's problems in recent years on the German political system. This would be a great injustice. Germany has enjoyed political stability and unparalleled economic success in Europe. The shortfalls of the additional member system there must be seen in the context both of these achievements and of the experiences of other countries using both proportional and non-proportional voting systems.

Box 4.5 Case study: elections to the Scottish Parliament

Since 1999, elections to the Scottish Parliament (and the Welsh Assembly) have used a variant of the additional member system. Like Germany, this has combined constituency-based simple plurality system contests as well as the regional party list. Unlike the German system, the two elements do not return equal numbers of representatives. The Scottish Parliament consists of 129 members. For the purpose of these elections, Scotland is broken up into eight regions, as illustrated by the map below.

Each of these regions elects seven MSPs (Members of the Scottish Parliament), making a total of fifty-six. The remaining seventy-three

Figure 4.5 Voting regions of Scotland

Table 4.9 The 2007 Scottish Parliament elections

Party	Constit-uencies	Regions	Seats +/-	Total
SNP	21	26	+20	47
Labour	37	9	-4	46
Conservative	4	13	-1	17
Lib Dem	11	5	-1	16
Greens	0	2	-5	2
Others	0	1	-2	1

After 73 of 73 constituencies declared

After 8 of 8 regions declared

MSPs are elected using the simple plurality system in single-member constituencies. This means there is a slight weighting towards the representation of constituency MSPs.

The ballot paper for elections to the Scottish Parliament is similar to the one shown to illustrate how the German system works, enabling voters to cast two votes, one for their constituency MSP and the other to elect MSPs from the lists drawn up by the political parties. Table 4.9 shows the results of the most recent elections, in 2007, to the Scottish Parliament.

Between 1999 and 2007, Scotland was governed by a coalition made up of the Labour Party and the Liberal Democrats. This government lost ground in 2007 and were four seats short of a bare majority in the election of that year. In the 2007 Scottish Assembly elections, the Scottish National Party was the single largest party, with 47 out of 129 seats. Clearly, this was not sufficient to form a majority government. Even after failing to secure the support of other parties to form a coalition government, the SNP decided to go it alone in the form of a minority government. This means that the Scottish government is at the mercy of the other parties in the Scottish Parliament, who could bring down the government if they joined together to vote against it in a confidence motion. Early in 2009, other political parties were threatening to vote against the government's budget proposals. If the government had failed to get its budget passed, then elections scheduled for 2011 would have been

> been brought forward. An accommodation was reached, however, and the threat of an early election was averted. Compromise either by parties in a coalition government or by a minority administration securing the support of opposition parties are clearly important elements in the working of the additional member system.

For more information on the outcome of elections to the Welsh Assembly, see Chapter 8.

Implications for governance and representation

The system combines proportionality with constituency representation. Furthermore, the constituencies are single-member ones, so it could be argued that the best of both the simple plurality system and the list system is achieved. Even if their chosen candidate has no chance of winning, at least voters have a party vote, which will go some way to help their chosen party.

The system has worked well in Germany, countering the critics who argue that proportional systems lead to weak and unstable governments. On the other hand, it may be argued that half of the MPs elected are not directly accountable to the electorate, who therefore have no effective constituency-based support. This means that there will effectively be two types of MP: one with constituency responsibilities (and therefore workload) and one without. In addition, the list-based element to this system once again gives the political parties a big say as to who will become an MP. A high threshold may lead to some very small parties finding themselves excluded from the Assembly despite polling hundreds of thousands of votes nationally. Many argue that the system would merely combine the worst aspects of the simple plurality system with the worst aspects of the list system, in other words candidates being elected in constituencies with under half of the total vote and voters having no say over which names appear in which position on the list.

The additional member system appears to answer many of the criticisms levelled at proportional representation in three ways: the link between the MP and constituent is maintained; it has an advantage over the single transferable vote because it does not involve a complicated counting process; and there is evidence from both abroad and within the UK to suggest that the system can sustain effective government in the long term and that there is not the calamitous instability associated with proportional systems. The British played a role in designing the German voting system in the late 1940s and this might have provided a clue about what system the UK will one day adopt for elections to the House of Commons. The Conservative–Liberal Democrat coalition might now change such assumptions.

There are still problems with the system, most notably to do with the party control of the lists and the level of the threshold, which, at 5 per cent in Germany, means that parties might poll hundreds of thousands of votes across the country but receive no representation. No system is going to be problem free. If there were such a system, the United Kingdom would probably already be using it.

AV+ Variation on a theme

Some critics of the additional member system argue that by using the simple plurality system for the constituency element of elections, there is still a possibility that the MP can be elected with less than half of the constituency vote. Although the national vote would be very largely proportional, a significant number of MPs might be elected without a proper mandate from their constituency electorate. A modified version of the additional member system, which would have effectively dealt with this criticism, was proposed in the late 1990s.

After his election victory in 1997, Tony Blair asked the former Home Secretary Lord Jenkins of Hillhead to investigate electoral systems which might be used to replace the simple plurality system for elections to the House of Commons. The Jenkins Commission report proposed a system called AV+ .[3]

Depending upon which system one adheres to, AV+ is either a variation of the alternative vote or an adapted version of the additional member system. The purpose of AV+ is to ensure both a proportional result and that every MP is returned with a majority of his or her electorate. The system is the same as the additional member system except that instead of the constituency vote being based on the simple plurality system, it relies instead on the alternative vote (a majority system examined in Chapter 3). The system would effectively ensure both majority representation in the constituencies and proportional representation in the country.

These proposals were rejected and there was never any further move on electoral reform for Westminster elections by Tony Blair's government. The promised referendum never materialised. Gordon Brown's government however did make late noises to suggest further interest in electoral reform. These noises were renewed after the 2010 general election and once more electoral reform, albeit not proportional representation, is back on the political agenda.

One constitutional change which might lead to electoral reform for some elections to the Westminster Parliament would be the introduction of an elected second chamber. All the political parties now favour at least some element of election. Indeed, the Conservative Party, long seen as defender of the House of Lords, now in coalition with the Liberal Democrats is committed to a fully or mainly elected second chamber. It is conceivable that such a chamber would be elected by proportional representation. This might lead to a constitutional dilemma for future governments. Britain could have a Parliament where the first, more powerful, chamber appears to be less representative and less legitimate than the second chamber. There could be talk of a new democratic deficit, where the least democratic institutions exercise the most power. It may be argued that once the 'genie' of electoral reform is let out of the bottle, it cannot be put back.

The United Kingdom may one day end up with a different electoral system. A number of systems have been examined in this and the previous two chapters. The relative merits of these systems can be discussed at length. Those whose criticism against electoral reform is a principled one will never be convinced of the merits of any system other than the simple plurality system. So while there may be answers to many of the problems associated with reform, a number of questions will inevitably remain. The question which needs to be addressed in these circumstances is whether the problems of any one system of reform outweigh those of the system we have already.

Proportional representation – a summary

Proportional representation is not a voting system, but a general term covering a number of systems which deliver seats to a party in proportion to the votes it receives. The notion of district magnitude will affect the proportionality of a voting system. The larger the area from which the representatives are being elected, the more proportional the result.

A list-based system which treats the whole country as one constituency is likely to provide a more proportional result than one where the list is broken into regions. The main drawback of the list system is the absence of constituency-based MPs. Critics of the list system claim that it further enhances the power of the party machine. Unless some effective threshold exists in a list system, very small parties could find themselves elected and able to wield considerable influence over government. Chapter 9 offers a fuller assessment of voting behaviour in elections to the European Parliament using the regional party list electoral system.

The single transferable vote combines proportionality and constituency representation. Supporters of the system argue that it empowers voters, giving them the right to choose between candidates of the same party.

STV offers citizens more than one MP (perhaps from different parties) from whom they may seek help and advice. Critics argue that the system lacks transparency and that it is unduly complicated. Some constituencies would by necessity be very large and difficult for MPs to maintain effective links. Chapter 8 offers a fuller assessment of voting behaviour in elections to the Northern Ireland Assembly using the single transferable vote electoral system.

It is claimed that the additional member system offers the best of all worlds, a proportional system with constituency representation that people will find easy to understand. Critics argue that it offers the worst of all worlds, with the list element of the system keeping the party leadership firmly in control and the first-past-the-post part of the system enabling many MPs to be elected without the approval of the majority of their constituents. The system has worked well in Germany since 1949 and has proved successful in Scotland and Wales since 1999. Despite critics' fears about PR, Germany has maintained a stable political system and a strong economy for much of this time. Chapters 6 and 7 offer a fuller assessment of voting behaviour in elections to the Scottish Parliament and the National Assembly for Wales using the additional member electoral system.

. . . .

What you should have learnt from reading this chapter

- An understanding of the essential features of proportional representation
- An understanding of the workings of different proportional systems
- A grasp of the main effects of proportional electoral systems
- An assessment of these electoral systems
- An assessment of the suitability of these systems for elections to the UK House of Commons

Glossary of key terms

Apparentement The provision of a list-based system where parties (usually smaller ones) may link their lists for the purposes of seat allocation. This maximises their chances of getting some representation.

Charter 88 An organisation at the forefront of campaigns to secure constitutional reform in Britain.

Dáil The name of the Parliament of the Republic of Ireland.

D'Hondt Formula The formula used for most list-based systems. It is used in the counting of votes in elections in Israel, for example, where a party's remaindered (or excess) votes are redistributed.

District magnitude This refers to the size of the electoral area and the number of representatives to be elected in that area. The bigger the electoral district and the more representatives that are elected to it, the larger the district magnitude is said to be. Normally, the larger the district magnitude, the more proportional the result is likely to be.

Droop Quota The formula which determines the number of votes required to win a seat in the single transferable vote system. The total number of votes cast is divided by the number of seats to be allocated, plus one. The resulting number is then increased by one to give the final figure.

Electoral Reform Society An organisation established to campaign for the replacement of the simple plurality electoral system with a system of proportional representation. The ERS has long campaigned for the adoption of the single transferable vote for use in UK general elections.

Good Friday Agreement Signed at Easter 1998, this agreement was the beginning of the political process in Northern Ireland that would bring power sharing between Catholics and Protestants after almost thirty years of violent conflict and a divided community. The agreement would pave the way for a referendum that would see over 70 per cent of voters support the new peace process and the setting up of new political institutions in Northern Ireland, including the Assembly.

Knesset The name of the single-chamber national assembly (Parliament) of Israel.

Mandate The authority given to a government to carry out its electoral promises. Some controversy exists about whether a party has a proper mandate if it has failed to poll at least 50 per cent of the vote.

Overhang In Germany, using the additional member system, a party may do so well in the constituencies that it ends up with a higher percentage of seats than votes. The party is allowed to keep those extra seats, and the overall size of the Bundestag is increased until the next election.

Proportional representation Not a system of voting but a collective term used to describe an electoral system in which the proportion of seats that a party obtains in an assembly matches the percentage of votes that that party receives.

Remaindered votes In list-based systems, it is likely that a party will obtain more than enough votes for, say, fifty seats, but not enough for fifty-one. The excess (or remaindered) votes over those needed for fifty seats can be reallocated to smaller parties that have linked up their lists in order to seek to maximise their allocation of seats (see Apparentement above).

Voting threshold In proportional systems, this is the minimum percentage vote that a party must achieve before being able to gain representation. In the German Bundestag, it is 5 per cent.

❓ Likely examination questions

What is proportional representation?

Outline the workings of three proportional electoral systems used in the United Kingdom.

To what extent do proportional electoral systems lead to weak and unstable government?

🖥 Helpful websites

The Electoral Reform Society

http://www.electoral-reform.org.uk/

Unlock Democracy (formerly Charter 88)

www.unlockdemocracy.org.uk/

Suggestions for further reading

P. Dunleavy, H. Margetts and S. Weir, *Replaying the 1992 General Election: How Britain Would Have Voted Under Alternative Electoral Systems*, LSE Public Policy Paper, no. 3, 1992.

D. Farrell, *Comparing Electoral Systems*, Prentice Hall, 2001.

M. Gallagher and P. Mitchell (eds), *The Politics of Electoral Systems*, Oxford University Press, 2005.

S. Henig and L. Baston, *Politico's Guide to the General Election 2005*, Politico's Publishing, 2005.

M. Soberg Shugart and M. P. Wattenberg, *Mixed-Member Electoral Systems*, Oxford University Press, 2003.

CHAPTER 5

Voting in UK General Elections

Contents

Overview

Voting behaviour in British general elections has been the subject of much published work. The main focus of this work has been on the changes to the forces that shape electoral behaviour among voters.

This chapter seeks to summarise the main characteristics of UK voting behaviour from the 1950s onwards and explain the extent and reasons for the changes in this after 1970.

Key issues to be covered in this chapter

- The main features of voting behaviour in the United Kingdom in the 1950s and 1960s
- The main explanations for voting behaviour in the 1950s and 1960s
- The main features of voting behaviour in the United Kingdom after 1970
- The main explanations for voting behaviour after 1970

General elections: the big picture

Voting in British general elections has changed dramatically in the past sixty years, moving from a time of two-party dominance to a position where, it would appear, only the simple plurality vote system is maintaining British politics in familiar shape. Later chapters will examine how the use of proportional voting systems in Scotland, Wales and Northern Ireland as well as in elections to the European Parliament has transformed the political dynamics of these institutions.

This chapter will examine the changes that have taken place in voting in general elections in Britain since the 1950s. Figure 5.1 provides an overview of general election results in the UK since 1945.

As can be seen from the figure, there has been a significant change in the fortunes of the main political parties over the sixty years. From a relatively stable period of two-party dominance, the UK became more of a three-party system, with major fluctuations of party support from one general election to another. This, then, is a story of political change. However, it may also be seen as a story of political inertia. Looking at data for the same series of elections in terms of

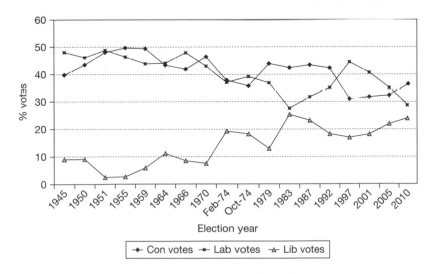

Figure 5.1 UK general elections 1945–2010 (votes)

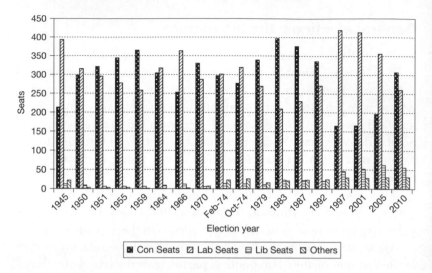

Figure 5.2 UK general elections 1945–2010 (seats)

House of Commons seats, this inertia becomes evident, as shown in Figure 5.2.

Although the representation of the smaller political parties has increased in recent elections, the main story here is one of the continued dominance of the Conservatives and Labour, far beyond what they have achieved in terms of votes.

Voting in the 1950s and 1960s

Two-party politics

British politics in the 1950s and the 1960s has been described as being 'two party' in nature, a period of political stability with voting behaviour being firmly anchored by a number of social alignments. Figure 5.3 gives an idea of the levels of political support during those years.

The chart clearly demonstrates the two-party label. The Liberals were well behind in single percentage support for virtually the whole period, while both Labour and the Conservatives enjoyed support that never fell below 40 per cent of the vote each. The stability of this two-party dominance has been the subject of much study, and some explanations of the phenomenon are offered later in this chapter.

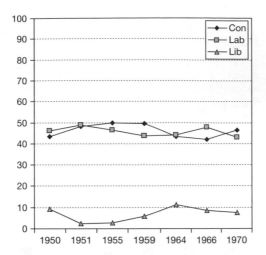

Statistics source: D. Butler and G. Butler, *British Political Facts 1900–1994,* Macmillan, 1994, pp. 216–17.

Figure 5.3 Party support in general elections 1950–70

If one was to aggregate the share of the vote enjoyed by Labour and the Conservatives, the scale of their dominance becomes apparent. The following pie chart (Figure 5.4) offers a powerful picture of this dominance averaged out over the twenty years between 1950 and 1970.

This overwhelming dominance of votes by the two main political parties meant that in the 1950s in particular, **third parties** were a virtual irrelevance. There was very little talk of electoral reform at this time. When it was discussed, it was largely confined to academic circles, with the Liberal Party in particular being unable to gain wider public sympathy for the issue.

Despite this, third parties were under-represented in the House of Commons during this period, however compared with the period after 1974, this was far less significant. Figure 5.5 indicates that even during this period there was not a perfect match between votes and seats for the Conservative and Labour parties.

This above data indicates that there is a disparity between the seats gained by each of the main parties and the number of votes obtained. In each case the disparity was large enough to maintain a government with a parliamentary majority without a majority of

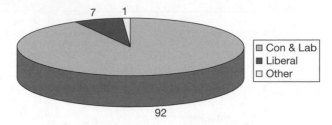

Figure 5.4 Average percentage vote in general elections 1950–70

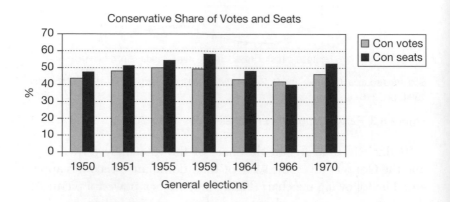

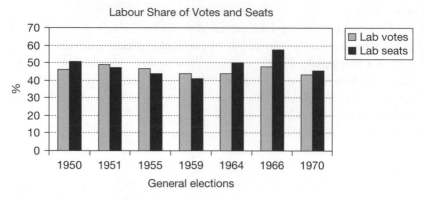

Adapted from election data in D. Butler and G. Butler, *British Political Facts 1900–1994*, Macmillan, 1994, pp. 216–17.

Figure 5.5 Conservative and Labour share of votes and seats in general elections 1950–70

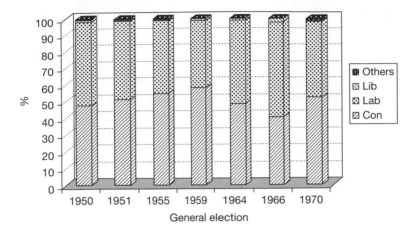

Adapted from election data in D. Butler and G. Butler, *British Political Facts 1900–1994*, Macmillan, London, 1994, pp. 216–17.

Figure 5.6 Percentage share of House of Commons seats 1950–70

votes. Clearly, the electoral system has never been perfect; however, the above anomalies are not nearly as serious as trends after 1970. This period also saw the chronic under-representation of the Liberal Party, although again, not to the extent of the 1970s onwards.

So even in the 1950s and 1960s, the simple plurality system could be accused of working against smaller parties, although it is probably more accurate to say that it really emphasised the dominance of the Conservative and Labour parties. In parliamentary terms this domination was almost complete. There were few Members of Parliament not taking the Conservative or Labour whip during this time.

Figure 5.6 shows the extent to which the two main parties dominated the House of Commons between 1950 and 1970.

It is almost impossible to see the seats occupied by Liberals and others because there were so few of them. During this period the combined share of the seats held by Labour and Conservative MPs never fell below 97 per cent.

Some commentators have interpreted the nature of the party system in the 1950s and 1960s in a somewhat different manner. Richard Rose offered numerous indicators to question whether the system was two-party in nature at all during this time. Other analyses characterise the period as one of a **dominant party** (the

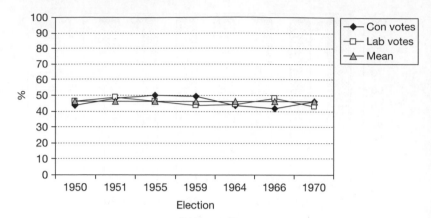

Figure 5.7 Two-party deviation from the mean 1950–70

Conservatives) with the period between 1964 and 1979 being some-what aberrant. Indeed, between 1951 and 1964 and again between 1979 and 1997, the British political system was dominated by the Conservatives.

Arguments such as these provide useful alternative interpreta-tions which remind us that a blind acceptance of the two-party description requires some qualification. However, this cannot deny the evidence that points towards that description as being accurate for the time. Indeed, between 1945 and 1979, both Labour and the Conservatives occupied the same time (approximately seven-teen years) in government. As indicated in the above charts, voting at general elections (the ones with the highest turnout) strongly indicated a two-party system and other indicative factors such as opinion polls and, to a lesser degree, **by-elections** all reinforce this analysis.

Political stability

What is also notable is the extent of political stability that existed during this time; this can be seen in Figure 5.7 which shows how little both political parties deviated from a statistical mean in the seven general elections of this period.

This compares with the situation after 1970, a foretaste of which is outlined in Figure 5.8 covering the subsequent seven general elec-tions between 1970 and 1997.

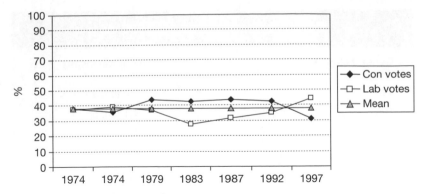

Figure 5.8 Two-party deviation from the mean 1974–97

Explaining voting behaviour 1950–70

How can the stable two-party political system of this time be explained? Nowadays many publications are based upon quantitative research methods. Previously, there was a lot of descriptive analysis of electoral behaviour, often emphasising it in terms of **rational voting**, stressing the role of the voter carefully weighing up the arguments over a range of issues before finally choosing a candidate or party to vote for. Typical of this is Viscount Bryce, who, writing shortly after the end of the First World War, described such a voter as 'the man of broad common sense, mixing on equal terms with his neighbours, forming a fair and unprejudiced judgement on every question'.[1]

Most books on the subject since the 1950s have been characterised by a more scientific and empirical approach. A new breed of experts emerged whose discipline was **psephology**. Research in the 1950s and 1960s both in Britain and the United States found major contradictions between voters' positions on issues and their party support. Successive opinion polls throughout the post-war period showed a disjuncture between Labour supporters and the party itself on issues such as capital punishment. These voters were certainly not acting rationally.

In the United States, *The American Voter*, the seminal work by Campbell et al., attempted to explode the myth of the rational voter,

Table 5.1 Electoral swing 1950–66

General election	Percentage swing
1950	2.9 to Con
1951	1.1 to Con
1955	1.8 to Con
1959	1.1 to Con
1964	3.1 to Lab
1966	2.7 to Lab

Data abstracted from P. Pulzer, *Political Representation and Elections in Britain*, George Allen & Unwin, 1975, p. 100.

offering in its place a model of voting behaviour which seemed better equipped to explain voter choice. On the question of voters carefully evaluating issues, they concluded, 'Many people fail to appreciate that an issue exists, others are insufficiently involved to pay attention to recognised issues, and still others fail to make connections between issue positions and party policy.' [2]

Furthermore, it has been found that over time attitudes were far from consistently held, with voters changing their minds on issues in significant numbers. Butler and Stokes found that on a number of key issues there was a major lack of consistency expressed. Surveys carried out using the same respondents in the early to mid 1960s showed a far from impressive level of consistency of opinion on issues such as nationalisation and Europe, leading the authors to conclude, 'It seems more plausible to interpret the fluidity of the public's views as an indication of the limited degree to which attitudes are formed towards even the best-known of policy issues.' [3]

The American Voter and, latterly, *Political Change in Britain* seriously questioned the impact that issues had on voting and showed that opinions on issues were highly volatile among those interviewed in surveys. The latter point is crucial, since in the 1950s and 1960s, voting behaviour remained very stable, as Table 5.1 illustrates.

In four of the elections, over half the constituencies had an **electoral swing** that was within 1 per cent of the national average.

This relatively consistent behaviour and stability of political support contrasts sharply with the volatility of attitudes to issues discussed earlier.

How can the apparent contradiction of relatively stable voting patterns and issue **volatility** be reconciled? If one wishes to stick to rational voter theory, the answer is simple – they can't. Other theories need to be examined. The studies of Campbell et al. in the United States and Butler and Stokes in Britain attempted to provide alternative explanations. David Denver creates a useful synthesis of much of this research. Of the 1950s and 1960s he writes:

> Broadly speaking, the electorate was divided into two large blocs which provided reliable and stable voting support for the Conservative and Labour parties. The interconnected phenomena of class and partisan alignment were the twin pillars . . . which supported and sustained stable party support on the part of individual voters and a stable two-party system overall.[4]

Class alignment

Research in the 1950s and 1960s in both Britain and the USA showed that of all the factors that might determine a person's voting behaviour (including gender, age, religion and regional locality) social class was by far the most accurate predictor. Put crudely, in Britain at this time, working-class people tended to vote Labour, while those from the middle class were overwhelmingly Conservative Party supporters.

The question of what actually constitutes class has long been fraught with difficulties. Should one's class be determined by income? If so, then at this time a coal miner, docker or steelworker would be middle class, given the more modest earnings of most office workers, many administrators and civil servants, who by implication would be working class. An added complication is that of so-called **self-assigned class**, where individuals perceived themselves as being in a particular social class without any objective justification for the claim.

Over the past ninety years, a measurement of social class has emerged which has become acceptable in both academic and commercial communities alike. This measurement is based upon occupation, and although it has been subject to some modification (and, it

Table 5.2 Social class and political party support

	1959		1964		1966		1970	
	nm	m	nm	m	nm	m	nm	m
Conservative	69	34	62	28	69	25	64	33
Labour	22	62	22	64	26	69	25	58
Liberal	8	4	8	14	14	6	11	9

nm = non-manual; m = manual
Adapted from D. Butler and D. Stokes, *Political Change in Britain*, Macmillan, 1974.

must be said, more recent challenge), it remains the most widely used measure of social class.

Most polling organisations, whether acting on behalf of the BBC, a national newspaper or a soap powder manufacturer, will base their research on one of a number of occupational measurements. The most frequently used measurement offers the following breakdown, based on the social classification of the Registrar General's Office:

A   Higher professional, managerial and administrative
B   Intermediate professional, managerial and administrative
C1 Supervisory clerical and other non-manual
C2 Skilled manual
D   Semi-skilled and unskilled manual
E   Residual and casual workers and people on state benefit

It is usual to speak in broad terms about social class, using the middle-class/working-class dichotomy. The middle class may be defined in terms of the three non-manual categories of the above list (grades ABC1). The working class may be identified by the manual groups (grades C2DE). During the 1950s and 1960s there appeared to be a close correlation between social class and support for political parties, as Table 5.2 illustrates.

To make more sense graphically, the figures from the above table have been averaged over the period and converted into graph form.

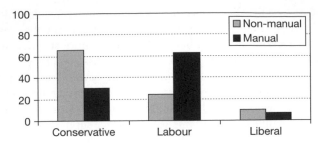

Figure 5.9 Class voting 1959–70

Figure 5.9 gives a much clearer idea of the scale of the nature of class-based voting.

At this point it should be noted that there is not a perfect match between social class and party support. Indeed, if one looks at the statistics for the manual working class during the period covered by the figure above, between a quarter and a third voted Conservative. The numbers of middle-class Labour supporters are more modest, but at between a fifth and a quarter during the period, they are far from insignificant. These **class-deviant voters** may be explained in a number of ways.

Explaining class-deviant voting

Middle-class supporters of the Labour Party were traditionally found in the professions rather than in business. Teachers, lecturers and doctors all had significant levels of support for Labour. This may be compared to managers in the business community who were over-whelmingly Conservative in nature. Working-class Conservatives were a crucial element of the two-party equation in the post-war years. Given that the working classes amounted to two-thirds of the voting population in the 1950s and 1960s, a party that was able to command all of this vote would have found itself in a permanent state of government. The presence of significant levels of working-class support for the Conservatives, however, meant that throughout this period, the Conservative and Labour parties had roughly half each of the popular support of the country. As such, the working-class Conservative has been of greater political significance and therefore also of greater academic interest. Peter Pulzer offers the following observation:

The Conservative Party has survived the democratization of the country by its ability to gain votes from the poor. For that reason the Tory working-man has been subjected to more study than the middle-class Socialist. While some middle-class sympathy may be important to the Labour Party in providing it with leadership and local organization, and perhaps also in confirming its claim to speak to the workers 'by hand and by brain', it does not have the statistical significance that the working-class support has for the Conservatives.[5]

How may one account for the phenomenon of the working-class Conservative? During the period under discussion, there were a number of explanations. The major one concerns the notion of social **deference**, where individuals perceive Conservative politicians as their betters and therefore suited to being leaders of the country.

The Conservatives have had more experience over the centuries. It's in the blood for them, running the country. There's more family background in the Conservatives, more of the aristocratic families, more heritage. They're gentlemen born. I think they're made for that sort of job.[6]

There are a number of alternative explanations for working-class Conservatism, including the impact of cross-pressures, where the membership of the working class is complicated by factors such as home ownership, or where voters may place themselves in the wrong social class. Detailed analysis of this phenomenon, however, is beyond the scope of this book.

Within these limitations, it remained the case that of all the possible influences that could affect voting behaviour, social class was by far the most important. Indeed, in 1967, Peter Pulzer's well-worn quotation-cum-academic soundbite summarised the position at the time rather well: 'Class is the basis of British party politics; all else is embellishment and detail.'[7]

If, as Pulzer declares, class was the basis of British party politics at this time, what was the basis for class voting? As can be seen from the first reference in this chapter to the work of Butler and Stokes, rational evaluation of issues does not appear to be the explanation. Indeed, given that they witnessed significant shifts of opinion from those they interviewed on important issues, one would have expected a more volatile, more changeable voting pattern if a widespread, rational connection had been made between opinions on issues and votes.

Perhaps class-based voting was rooted in a more general perception about which party was most likely to defend the interests of certain groups with which individuals identified, rather than careful evaluation of specific issues. In other words, the Labour Party was seen by the majority of the working class as the party most likely to look after them in such areas as employment and welfare. Conversely, the middle class shared the broad Conservative beliefs in social hierarchy, defence of traditional values and the importance of the creation and conservation of wealth. Furthermore, the middle class felt hostility to the Labour Party, in that it was perceived that Labour would somehow 'hurt' their class interests.

Partisan alignment

Party identification was first established as an important phenomenon in helping explain voting behaviour in the 1950s. The authors of *The American Voter* described it as 'a psychological attachment to party, varying in direction and intensity'.[8]

What this means is that voters do not simply vote for a political party on a momentary whim, but that they hold an enduring bond with a political party (in the case of the United States, either Democrat or Republican). This bond could be strong, moderately strong or weak, but the stronger the party identification, the stronger the bond and consequently the more durable a voter's loyalty to a party. Butler and Stokes, when conducting their own research into the phenomenon in Britain, found that during this time, levels of party identification were high: 'in 1963 well over four-fifths of our respondents said they had always supported the same party'.[9]

This indicates a great level of stability from one election to another in those days. Voters more readily accepted the labels 'Labour', 'Conservative' and 'Liberal' being attached to them. People did not simply vote Conservative, they saw themselves *as* Conservatives.

Voters, it seemed, were willing to be classified in this way. Table 5.3, adapted from Crewe, demonstrates this very clearly.

Throughout the 1960s, nine out of ten voters identified with

Table 5.3 Level of party identification 1964–70

	1964	1966	1970
% with party identification	93	91	90
% identifying with Con	38	35	40
% identifying with Lab	43	46	42

Table adapted from I. Crewe, 'Partisan dealignment ten years on', in D. Denver and G. Hands, *Issues and Controversies in British Electoral Behaviour*, Prentice Hall/ Harvester Wheatsheaf, 1992, p. 143.

Table 5.4 Strength of party identification 1964–70

	1964	1966	1970
% very strong identifiers	44	44	42
% fairly strong identifiers	38	38	37
% not very strong identifiers	11	9	11
non-identifiers	7	9	10

Table adapted from I. Crewe, 'Partisan dealignment ten years on', in D. Denver and G. Hands, *Issues and Controversies in British Electoral Behaviour*, Prentice Hall/Harvester Wheatsheaf, 1992, p. 143.

one of the political parties, and eight out of ten identified with either Labour or the Conservatives. As previously mentioned, it was not merely the level of party identification that was noted, but the strength of partisanship was also observed. This may be seen in Table 5.4.

By adding together the very strong and fairly strong identifiers, it may be seen that during the 1960s, consistently more than 80 per cent of the electorate had at least a fairly strong attachment to their chosen political party.

Clearly, the strength of **partisanship** during this time helps explain the stable two-party system during the 1960s. Recall data collected by Butler and Stokes from the time of the 1959 general election offers findings consistent with the notion that strong partisanship was a major force shaping electoral behaviour during the 1950s and 1960s. The electorate displayed great loyalty to their chosen party at this time, the strength of which appears to have been decisive in maintaining consistency in voting behaviour. Even when individuals did change their vote, it was often the case that they maintained their party identification with their original party. In other words, party identification tended to endure even when party support in elections changed.

Party identification may be seen almost as a psychological anchor, which moors a voter's allegiance to a political party, even when that party may be enduring political problems. This resulted in an era where the main parties were able to hold on to the bulk of their supporters even during or after very difficult times. By the 1970s, however, the picture began to look very different.

Electoral trends after 1970

After the 1970 general election, the stability of the 1950s and 1960s seemed to disappear. The general election of February 1974 resulted in the first minority government in Britain since 1929. The February election also saw not only a fall in support for the Heath government, but also a corresponding decline in the vote of Wilson's Labour opposition. The smaller political parties claimed that neither Labour nor the Conservatives were able to claim a right to govern Britain and the success of nationalist parties in Scotland and (to a lesser extent) in Wales put further pressure on a political system whose governing party (Labour) was elected to office with nearly a quarter of a million fewer votes than the Conservatives who had lost on seats.

It had been common to describe the British political system as two-party in nature and with Labour and the Conservatives able to obtain nine out of every ten votes cast in the 1950s and 1960s, this description appeared to be appropriate. The Liberal Party was virtually an electoral irrelevance in the 1950s and its average level of support in general elections in the 1960s remained below 10 per cent. By 1974, Labour and the Conservatives were able to achieve 75 per cent of the vote between them, compared with the 98 per cent they achieved in 1951.

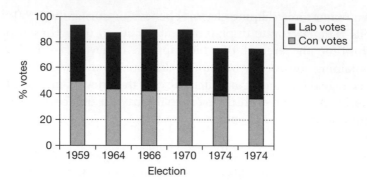

Figure 5.10 Combined Conservative and Labour share of votes 1959–74

Support for the two main political parties thus declined dramatically in the early 1970s, as may be seen in Figure 5.10.

The result of the general election of May 1979 led many to believe that the two-party system had clicked back into place. Indeed, the new Conservative government had a healthy majority and no one questioned its ability to carry on for a full five-year term. The Liberal Party seemed to have peaked and its support fell back sharply. The nationalist tide appeared to have turned and the much-heralded rise of the far right failed to materialise.

In fact, the 1979 result was further evidence that political certainties were crumbling. The Conservative victory saw the biggest swing of any election since the Second World War. Furthermore, the swing was most prominent among skilled working-class voters, the so-called C2s. It would appear that the volatility which resulted in the minority governments of the 1970s was still causing political upheaval and fuelling a variety of political outcomes.

Certainly the combined share of the vote for Labour and the Conservatives increased in 1979, but only up to just over 80 per cent, a far cry from a generation before when the percentage figure was up in the 90s. Indeed, if we look at the figures for 1983, 1987, 1992 and even the landslide of 1997, it may be seen that at no time does this combined share of the vote rise above 80 per cent. By the 2005 and 2010 general elections, the combined share of the vote enjoyed by Labour and the Conservatives had fallen below 70 per cent.

Box 5.1 The issue of electoral reform

By the 1970s, therefore, the issue of electoral reform was being looked upon in a different light. The Liberals had polled just under a fifth of the national vote and could have expected over 100 extra seats from a proportional system. No longer could the overwhelming electoral dominance of the two main political parties be used to dismiss calls for electoral reform. For perhaps the first time since the 1920s it appeared that the main political players were being propped up by a voting system which was denying a voice to millions of voters and suppressing the representation of other political parties.

The elections of 1974 not only brought the Liberals into the forefront of the British political system. Other political forces also stirred at this time, notably the nationalist movement in Scotland. During the 1960s, both the Scottish National Party and the Welsh nationalists, Plaid Cymru, had scored notable by-election successes. Plaid Cymru's support peaked at just over 175,000 votes in the 1970 general election, but in the elections of 1974 the SNP was able to poll up to 30 per cent of the Scottish vote.

In October 1974, the SNP won eleven seats in the House of Commons, and although polling over 800,000 votes in Scotland, this only represented 2.9 per cent of the vote in the United Kingdom as a whole. Compare this with the Liberals, who in 1955 polled just over 700,000 votes, constituting 2.7 per cent of the total, resulting in 6 seats. A comparison between the Liberals and the SNP in October 1974 makes interesting reading, as Table 5.5 illustrates.

Clearly, not all minor political parties are affected by the simple plurality electoral system in the same way. Although the SNP would have been likely to benefit from around eight extra seats under some

Table 5.5 Liberal and SNP support in the October 1974 general election

Party	Seats	% votes	% seats
Liberal	13	18.3	2.0
Scottish National Party	11	2.9	1.7

Extracted from D. E. Butler and G. Butler, *British Political Facts 1900–1994*, Macmillan Press, 1994.

form of proportional voting, this hardly compares to the extra 100 seats that the Liberals would have won.

A party fielding relatively few candidates in a nationally and culturally specific region is likely to be able to amass a relatively modest number of votes per candidate fielded and still win a respectable percentage of the seats fought. In October 1974, the SNP fought in seventy constituencies in Scotland, with eleven candidates winning seats, a 16 per cent success rate. The Liberals fielded 619 candidates across the UK, but only achieved success in 13 constituencies, a 2 per cent success rate.

Political parties with popular support very thinly distributed across the country (such as the Liberal Democrats even today) are likely to fare less well than a party with relatively concentrated support, such as nationalist parties like the SNP and traditionally, to an extent, both Labour and the Conservatives.

Explaining political volatility after 1970

How may the sudden decline in support for the Conservatives and Labour in the early 1970s and the rise in the fortunes of third parties be explained? What was the reason for Conservative dominance in the 1980s? Why did Labour make such a miraculous recovery in the 1990s? It may be argued that all these seemingly conflicting phenomena were in fact the result of the same political and electoral forces.

Earlier in the chapter, an attempt was made to explain stable two-party voting using the concepts of class alignment and partisan alignment. Political parties were able to weather many a storm and still retain their support, largely intact. Of course parties lost as well as won elections, but the swings were never great. The two main parties appeared to take it in turns to run the country. Third parties might score the odd success at **by-elections**, but nothing more.

If it were not for the simple plurality voting system, it is likely that the political shifts of opinion that took place after 1970 would have had a greater and much more immediate impact on government in Britain. As it was, despite losing millions of votes between them, Labour and the Conservatives attempted to carry on as they had done in the previous two decades.

In the late 1970s, important research was published which seemed

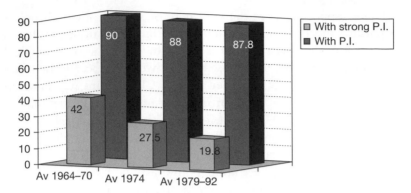

Adapted from D. Denver, *Elections and Voting Behaviour in Britain*, 2nd edn, Harvester Wheatsheaf, 1994, p. 54.

Figure 5.11 Party identification 1964–92

to indicate that weaknesses in the old alignments were appearing. Indeed, the origins of these changes went back to when the so-called 'era of alignment' was in full swing (see below). It was after 1970 that the effects of these changes could be seen.

In two key areas of class and partisanship, changes appeared to be taking place. The era of alignment seemed to have given way to the era of dealignment; in other words, a weakening of party identification and social class as the major influences was taking place.

Partisan dealignment

Earlier in this chapter, it was shown that nine out of ten voters identified with a political party and that just over four in ten had a very strong attachment to 'their' party. By contrast, in the 1980s and 1990s the picture had changed. Voters still tended to identify with a particular party in similar numbers, but the strength of this identification appeared to have weakened significantly. Figure 5.11 offers a picture of the changes.

People still identified themselves with a particular political party. They were, however, unable to commit themselves strongly. This latter figure more than halved over the period being discussed. As it is strong identifiers who are likely to be the more enduring in terms of their willingness to turn out and vote for the same party, elections are bound to be affected by such a decline.

These supporters were the very core of support for both political parties, and their number appears to have diminished. What is left seems to be a mass of voters who can make the psychological attachment to a party, but whose support would appear to be more conditional on a range of other factors. Clearly, this will have an impact upon parties at election time because a strong identifier is less likely to be swayed by events or crises than someone whose partisanship is weaker. Consequently, the more weaker identifiers there are, the greater potential there is for other factors to influence them. The simple plurality system appears to mask these trends. The two main parties still dominate seats in the House of Commons. In the following chapters it will be seen that once this electoral system is stripped away and replaced with a more proportional one, the political choices of the electorate become reflected in a much more diverse representation of political parties.

Reasons for the weakening of partisanship

Heightened political awareness combined with an electorate that has become increasingly cynical with main political parties appear to have eroded the strength of party identification over time.

Perhaps the electorate is more aware of issues and more willing to be affected by them. Following the expansion of the university sector in the early 1960s and the continued growth in higher education since then, there may be a case for suggesting that overall levels of education have affected voter loyalties. Crewe, Sarlvik and Alt (1977) have suggested that in the period of their study (1964–74), it was among those with higher education qualifications that the greatest decline in the strength of partisanship had taken place.[10]

A more educated electorate may be able to weigh up issues in a more objective fashion and be less likely to have formed an emotional relationship with a single political party. If the relationship between a voter and a party can be explained more rationally, this then might account for the increasingly conditional nature of the relationship the former has with the latter.

From the 1970s, the increasing population of students in higher education would not be sufficient to explain the major electoral and political changes that were going on at this time. There are other sources of information about politics. Newspapers, for example, don't just offer political information; they also offer views and comment. To what extent can this influence voters? What about the impact of television?

It was not until the general election of 1959 that there was the sort of television coverage that we might recognise today. Even then, the tone of, say, Richard Dimbleby was far more deferential than we would expect today from either of his sons, David and Jonathan, or indeed Jeremy Paxman. In the 1960s, the likes of Robin Day and David Frost adopted a more interrogatory style and turned the political interview into more of a trial by television.

Politicians are now seen differently, their weaknesses exposed for millions to see, their policies put under the spotlight and their arguments scrutinised for inconsistencies. Gone are the days when a party leader could effectively determine the conduct and outcome of a television interview and it could be argued that, over time, this may have had an impact upon the perceptions of the millions watching.

The lack of deference towards our political leaders also broadened into popular culture. In the early 1960s, the satirical magazine *Private Eye* was launched and has thrived ever since on a diet of lampoon, political gossip and investigative journalism. Television was no stranger to this phenomenon. *That Was The Week That Was* featured many sketches aimed at deflating the importance of the political elite. Since then, the likes of *Spitting Image* in the 1980s and more recently impressionists such as Rory Bremner and John Culshaw and radio programmes such as *The Now Show* have depicted politicians as a dishonest and venal bunch (a portrayal not helped, of course, by the MPs' expenses furore in 2009).

On its own, however, all this is not enough to decrease partisan strength. For a satirist to be guaranteed of a laugh, he or she must strike a chord with the audience. If politicians were doing everything right, then there would probably be no satirists. If the sketches of the satirists are to ring true, political parties must have been doing something wrong in the first place. Over the past forty years, our political parties have been promising to deliver the people from bad times (usually caused by the previous government of the opposing party) to better ones. Governments always seem to leave office having failed in the eyes of the voters.

In some respects this is the result of a combination of factors.

Politicians have spent much of this time promising better times and voters have come to have increasing expectations of what politicians can do. In the 1950s, with a growing economy and years of relative prosperity, governments were able to deliver on promises. Hospitals were opened, schools were replaced and council houses were built. By the 1960s, however, this era was over, with the country facing economic problems, such as unemployment, balance of payments difficulties and inflation. These problems were often experienced in turn and occasionally at the same time. Unfortunately, however, the politicians still promised and the voters still expected. It became only a matter of time before an increasing number of voters realised that neither party in office was delivering what they said they would do while in opposition.

Labour was particularly badly hit early in this 'era of dealignment'. Between 1970 and 1997, the party was in power for just over five years. The Conservatives, by contrast, were in power for eighteen consecutive years. Were there forces at work which were particularly harmful to Labour? Was it these forces with which Labour battled between 1983 and 1997? By shifting its position in key policy areas, was Labour able to turn these forces to its own advantage?

There is evidence to suggest that an increasing number of voters (including Labour ones) were becoming increasingly disaffected by traditional socialist policies such as nationalisation and trade union power.[11]

The reasons for this may be inextricably linked with changes in social class. Clearly, following their electoral defeat in 1983, Labour could have chosen one of two directions in which to travel: first, it could have continued along the road on which it had started out, at the beginning of the 1980s, waiting for the 'inevitable' crisis in capitalism; alternatively, it could begin the journey back to the centre ground in the hope of recapturing its lost support.

Labour chose the latter course and in so doing, it has been claimed, abandoned everything it stood for. The rights and wrongs of what happened are for a different debate; clearly, however, in the long term, the party managed to overcome some of the negative stereotypes which some believe kept it out of government for so long. Labour's large army of party identifiers had diminished to the extent that it had to make a major re-evaluation of its purpose and policy in order to have a chance at returning to government.

Class dealignment

Earlier in this chapter the relationship between a person's vote and their social class was examined. There was general agreement that it was the single most significant factor in the 1950s and 1960s. There were so-called 'class-deviant voters' and indeed, given the relative size of the working and middle classes, the Conservative Party can be thankful for these, otherwise it is likely that they would have been continuously out of office in the first decades after the Second World War.

Was there a breakdown in the relationship between social class and vote after 1970? In 1964, Labour had the support of 64 per cent of the working-class vote. By 1983 this had fallen to 42 per cent. The Conservatives did not fare as badly: in the same period their share of the middle-class vote fell by only 7 per cent (from 62 per cent to 55 per cent). So there was change and this seemed to affect Labour more than the Conservatives.

There are other ways of measuring the change in class voting. Perhaps the best known is the **Alford Index**, which is calculated by simple subtraction. For Labour, one can simply subtract the party's percentage share of the middle class (non-manual workers) from its share of the working class (manual workers). So if Labour has 66 per cent of the working-class support and only 25 per cent of the middle-class support, then its index is forty-one. The higher the figure (up to a maximum of 100), the greater the degree of class voting. The Conservative figures are calculated the opposite way round (by deducting the percentage of working-class share of the vote from the middle-class share of the vote).

Between 1964 and 1983, Labour's Alford Index score fell from forty-two to twenty-five (a fall of 40 per cent), while the Conservative score fell from thirty-four to twenty (a 41 per cent fall) over the same period. The figures flatten out after the 1980s and 1990s. Clearly, therefore, there was a decline in class voting during the 1960s and 1970s. By the 1980s, social class was no longer the predictor that it had once been and this continues to be the case.

What were the reasons for the desertion of so many voters from their natural party of class? Were these desertions temporary or a more permanent feature? Where were the new homes of these votes and could they be relied upon to stay put?

Reasons for class dealignment

Some of the reasons used to explain the weakening of partisanship can also help explain the reasons for class dealignment and vice versa. The debate over the weakening of the influence of social class is not a new one, however. In the 1960s, Goldthorpe et al. attempted to measure the impact of working-class affluence among Luton car workers upon Labour Party support. (The resulting book was entitled *The Affluent Worker.*) They found no evidence at the time that this affluence was likely to lead to the abandonment of the Labour Party.

By the 1980s, however, there would appear to be some greater claim that affluence was an important factor. By this time, many more working-class people owned their own homes, owned a car (or even two), owned shares and took foreign holidays. While it is not suggested that owning a house will turn a person into a natural Conservative voter, it will perhaps make the 'property-owning, share-owning democracy' message of the Conservatives in the 1980s more resonant to a greater number of people, the working class included.

The above point may offer some indication why some working-class people have been willing to desert the Labour Party, but what about the middle class and the Conservatives? It seems doubtful that in a period of increasing affluence, where working-class voters are discovering the merits of a market economy, members of the middle class are deserting this cause for Labour and the Liberals. The structure of the middle class has changed, however. It is no longer the preserve of bankers, solicitors, clerks and doctors. In the 1960s and 1970s, there was a huge growth in public-sector professionals (teachers, social workers, educational psychologists, lecturers and so on). A large proportion of this group of workers will have had a natural 'communion of interest' with the left in British politics, and the Labour Party is probably where many would offer their support. In addition, this group also had a natural affinity with the public sector in which they worked, a sector popularly associated with the Labour Party. The massive growth in the size of the public sector when Labour is in power is perhaps evidence of this.

David Denver argues that there are three trends worthy of note when examining the issue of social class and voting:

- A shift from manual to non-manual work
- A shift from manufacturing to the service sector
- Within manufacturing, a particularly severe decline in traditional, heavy industries, such as steel, coal and shipbuilding[12]

Patrick Dunleavy has suggested that the old occupational cleavage of manual/non-manual workers is becoming less important. The old class system is being replaced by a new one, based upon one's position in the public and private sector. This is known as **sectoral cleavage**. According to this theory, an individual working in the public sector whose children go to state schools and whose family are reliant upon state benefits is more likely to support the Labour Party than a person working and consuming predominantly in the private sector (owning their own home, sending children to private schools and having private healthcare).

This picture is further complicated by those who do not conform to a stereotypical working- or middle-class set of characteristics. It may be that a person has a manual job but owns his or her own home. It may be that a couple live in council accommodation, with the husband working in a manual occupation and the wife in a non-manual job. It may be argued that as increasing numbers of people are affected by the forces of more than one social class, the influence of either one of them is likely to be diluted.

Even within a social class there may be differences that are likely to have an impact upon political behaviour. Crewe, writing in the early 1980s, argued that within the working class, two distinct camps can be discerned: a traditional working class, characterised by those in public-sector manual jobs, living in a council house in the north; and a new working class of manual workers in the private sector, in their own homes in the south. It has been argued that in the former group, support for the Labour Party remained strong but in the latter group this support was much weaker.

In the 1980s and 1990s, such points were often used as part of Labour Party obituaries, in explanation of how and why the party would meet its eventual end. These obituaries were somewhat premature. Indeed, the revival of Labour's fortunes at the end of the

1990s was accomplished by tapping into the reserves of working-class voters who owned their own homes, had shares in British Telecom and worked in the private sector.

Indeed, part of the Labour Party's success in 1997 and 2001 was in being able not only to recapture the votes of those who had deserted them for Margaret Thatcher in 1979, but also to attract those who had never voted Labour before in their lives. In this respect it was the Conservatives who suffered the mass desertion.

The collapse in the support for the Labour Party after 2005 is evidence that voters of all classes are willing to shift their votes elsewhere, including to parties such as the British National Party and the United Kingdom Independence Party.

The old certainties about class and vote have become very unreliable predictors of voting intentions. The quote from Peter Pulzer, cited earlier in the chapter, that anything other than class was 'embellishment and detail', comes to mind. In the forty years since he wrote those words, the relationships between individuals and social class have become too complex to generalise and difficult to explain in terms of voting behaviour.

Volatility

The word volatility has been used on numerous occasions in this chapter; however, the term 'voter volatility' has not been used as there is some debate in academic circles as to the extent of this. Pippa Norris suggests that there was indeed voter volatility in Britain in the early 1970s, but that after this time there were no trends that could be discerned. Rather, there were 'trendless fluctuations' which could be observed in the late 1970s and throughout the 1980s.[13] To some extent the 1997 general election offered the best evidence for a volatile electorate since the early 1970s, the swing from the Conservatives to Labour being the biggest by far since 1945.[14]

The periods between 1979 and 1992 and those after 1997 might be seen to fly in the face of the idea of volatility. If one examines some of the shifts in votes during these periods, one may think again. Labour lost millions of votes in 1983 and again in 2005.

Perhaps the term 'political volatility' should be used to indicate a phenomenon that is wider than voting behaviour. Simply limiting one's analysis of volatility to the size of electoral swings when a relatively small swing could have such a major impact on the distribution of seats in the House of Commons in the 1980s and 1990s is too narrow in focus.

Furthermore, the era has been characterised by major social, economic and political change. The effects of the United Kingdom's membership of the European Union, the major economic upheavals of the 1970s and 1980s and the changes in the political parties are all bound to have made a significant impact on the behaviour of voters and politicians alike.

The major constitutional developments introduced from the late 1990s have provided the opportunity for voters to elect their Euro MPs and devolved assembly representatives using systems of proportional representation. If the political changes outlined in this chapter are enduring, then these assemblies should show a marked divergence of representation compared to the House of Commons. The following four chapters examine voting in the elections to the devolved assemblies in Scotland, Wales and Northern Ireland as well as to the European Parliament.

. . . .

What you should have learnt from reading this chapter

- An understanding of voting patterns in the United Kingdom in the 1950s and 1960s
- The factors explaining voting behaviour in the 1950s and 1960s
- An understanding of voting patterns in the United Kingdom after 1970
- The factors explaining voting behaviour after 1970

Glossary of key terms

Alford Index A way of measuring class voting. The calculation works for either Labour or the Conservatives. For Labour, deduct the party's percentage share of non-manual workers from its share of manual workers (the range is 0–100; in other words, if all Labour voters were manual workers, then the calculation would be 100 − 0 = 100).

By-election In Britain, an election that takes place in a constituency where a vacancy has arisen due to either the death, resignation or disqualification of a Member of Parliament or other elected representative.

Class-deviant voters Voters who do not support their natural party of class – for example, working-class Conservatives and middle-class Labour supporters.

Deference Attitude of those who support a political party mainly in the belief that the leaders of that party are in some way their betters. It is most commonly applied to working-class voters supporting the Conservative Party in the 1950s and 1960s.

Dominant party Where one party dominates the political agenda over a long period of time. Other parties then experience long periods of opposition. It may be argued that Britain had a system dominated by the Conservatives between 1979 and 1997.

Electoral swing The shift in votes between the political parties from one election to the next, usually expressed in percentage terms.

Partisanship (also known as party identification). More than simply voting for a party, this is a psychological attachment to a political party, which may vary in strength. It is argued that in the 1950s and 1960s, partisan alignment was one of the anchors of the stable two-party system.

Psephology The study of elections and voting behaviour.

Rational voting Where voters carefully evaluate all sides of an argument or issue before casting their vote. This assumes that voters can make informed judgements about a range of policies and accurately identify the stances taken on these issues by the main political parties.

Sectoral cleavages The idea that the old cleavage or division in society based on occupation (or social class) has been replaced by a new division between those who work and consume in the public sector and those who work and consume in the private sector. Clearly, it is unlikely that there are many who fit this division 100 per cent, but it is argued that a public-sector worker living in a council house is more likely to support the Labour Party than is a private-sector worker who is an owner-occupier.

Self-assigned class Where an individual classifies himself into a particular social class. This is based upon the perception that voters have of themselves.

Third parties A term used to describe parties other than Labour and the Conservatives.

Volatility It may be argued that after the political stability of the 1950s and 1960s, the British political system became more volatile. There appeared to be large shifts in votes in 1979, and large shifts in seats in both 1983 and 1997. The evidence for electoral instability, however, lacks consistency.

? Likely examination questions

Distinguish between class alignment and partisan alignment.

'The two-party system in Britain is dead.' Discuss.

Helpful websites

Student test materials

http://www.educationforum.co.uk/sociology_2/votes.htm

Danny Dorling, *Class Alignment*, University of Sheffield, EPOP Conference Paper, September 2005

http://www.essex.ac.uk/bes/EPOP%202005/Papers/ DorlingClassAlignmentPaper.pdf

Suggestions for further reading

D. Butler and G. Butler, *British Political Facts 1900–1994*, Macmillan, 1994.

D. Butler and D. Stokes, *Political Change in Britain*, Macmillan, 1974.

A. Campbell, P. Converse, W. Miller and D. Stokes, *The American Voter*, John Wiley & Sons, Inc., 1960.

I. Crewe, 'Partisan dealignment ten years on', in D. Denver and G. Hands, *Issues and Controversies in British Electoral Behaviour*, Prentice Hall/ Harvester Wheatsheaf, 1992.

I. Crewe, B. Sarlvik and J. Alt, 'Partisan Dealignment in Britain 1964–1974', *British Journal of Political Science*, vol. 7, no. 2 (1977), pp. 129–90.

D. Denver, *Elections and Voting Behaviour in Britain*, Prentice Hall/ Harvester Wheatsheaf, 1994.

P. Pulzer, *Political Representation and Elections in Britain*, George Allen & Unwin, 1975.

CHAPTER 6

Voting in Scotland

Contents

Overview

The Blair government held a referendum on Scottish devolution in 1997. The result was a convincing 'Yes' vote, and the outcome is that Scotland has elected its own Parliament since 1999. As part of the new constitutional settlement in Scotland, the new Parliament has been elected using a different electoral system from the one that Scots use to elect MPs to the House of Commons.

This chapter explores the differences between Scottish voting in general elections and in those for the devolved Parliament. In addition, there will be an examination of the fortunes of the main political parties in Scotland and finally an assessment of how the additional member system of voting has affected the outcome of the devolved elections in Scotland.

Key issues to be covered in this chapter

- The background to Scottish voting behaviour
- The distinction between Scottish and Westminster elections
- How the main political parties have fared in devolved elections
- An assessment of the additional member electoral system

Background

Since the 1950s, the Labour Party has dominated the Scottish political system, at least as far as Scotland's MPs in the House of Commons are concerned. The Conservative Party, once a major political force north of the border, was reduced to a small rump of MPs by the 1980s and was wiped out by 1997, having lost its last constituency in Scotland.

As far as the other parties are concerned, the Liberals (now the Liberal Democrats) have traditionally been strong in the Scottish borders and the Highlands. Most of the seats in Scotland are concentrated in the Central Lowland region, where most of Scotland's population live, and this is where the Labour Party has tightened its grip for over fifty years. Many Labour politicians have assumed throughout their political careers that their party was *the* party of Scotland.

The previous chapter offered an analysis of the long-term factors affecting voting behaviour. There is some evidence that these endured longer in Scotland than in England. Indeed, the 1979 general election result seemed to see the emergence of a north-south divide in the support for political parties, and Scotland was the only part of the United Kingdom where Labour's share of the vote actually increased. Indeed, the trend was most pronounced when comparing constituency results in the south of England with those in Scotland. Scotland, it seemed, preferred to hold on to Labour, which stressed its commitment to public spending and welfare, whereas England preferred the lure of tax cuts and home ownership. Partisan dealignment seems to have affected those in the south more than those in Scotland and the north of England.

From the late 1960s, however, a new force, the Scottish National Party (SNP), began to make real inroads. In 1967, they had won their first Westminster seat after a by-election victory in Hamilton. This was followed by by-election wins in rock-solid Labour areas such as Glasgow Govan in the early 1970s. In the February 1974 general election, the SNP won twelve seats and the issue of Scotland's part in the Union became a major debate.

Indeed, it may be argued that it was because of the threat from the SNP that the Labour governments of Harold Wilson and James

Table 6.1 Party breakdown (%) in Scottish House of Commons seats 1970–9

Party	1970	Feb 1974	Oct 1974	1979
Con	32.4	29.6	22.5	31.0
Lab	62.0	56.3	57.8	62.0
Lib	4.2	4.2	4.2	4.2
SNP	1.4	9.9	15.5	2.8

Source: http://www.psr.keele.ac.uk/psr.htm

Callaghan (1974–9) attempted to create a devolved Parliament for Scotland. There was a view that many people in Scotland wanted greater autonomy from Westminster, but that they would settle for something short of full independence. In a sense, therefore, critics of devolution might argue that it is a sop to the Scots as well as a way of undermining nationalist support.

There was, of course, another reason why Labour was fundamentally opposed to independence. As mentioned above, by the 1970s Labour dominated the Scottish seats in the House of Commons. Table 6.1 shows the percentage breakdown of parties among Scottish seats from 1970 to 1979.

As can be seen, Labour's share of the seats never fell below 56 per cent. The true significance of these figures can only be seen when comparing them with the parties' share of seats in England. These figures are shown in Table 6.2 below.

This table shows a very different picture. Here we see Labour's share of English seats sharply decline after the two general elections of 1974. Indeed, if we look at the elections between 1964 and 1979, in three out of the four that Labour won, it failed to register a majority of English seats in the House of Commons. It is clear, therefore, that without Scotland's Labour MPs (and those from Wales) Labour would not have been able to form a government.

The election victories in 1997 and 2001 were certainly helped by Scottish MPs, but these victories were also the product of big electoral swings in England, so Labour could have won, albeit more

Table 6.2 Party breakdown (%) in English House of Commons seats 1970–9

Party	1970	Feb 1974	Oct 1974	1979
Con	57.1	51.7	48.8	59.3
Lab	42.3	45.9	49.4	39.3
Lib	0.4	1.7	1.5	1.4

Source: http://www.psr.keele.ac.uk/psr.htm

narrowly, in these elections. An examination of the 2005 general election, however, tells a different story. Here there was a swing away from Labour, and in addition the number of Scottish MPs was reduced from seventy-two to fifty-nine. Both these factors contributed to Labour's slump in support in 2005.

The extent of SNP success should not be overstated. At no point from the 1970s through to the beginning of the devolved Scottish Parliament did the party achieve more than 20 per cent of Scotland's Westminster seats. Indeed, the moves made to bring devolved government to Scotland were made in the absence of the SNP and were contrived by the Scottish Labour Party and the Scottish Liberal Democrats. By 1995, both parties jointly published their proposals in a document entitled 'Scotland's Parliament, Scotland's Right'.

There was one major sticking point which had previously divided the Scottish Labour Party and the Scottish Liberal Democrats and that was the voting system that would be employed for electing the new Scottish Parliament. The Scottish Liberal Democrats had long favoured the single transferable vote system (see Chapter 4) but many in the Scottish Labour Party were firmly opposed to any change in the simple plurality system. This latter view was based on straightforward party political advantage. Labour was dominant in terms of Scottish seats, but the figures are not so clear when one looks at the distribution of Scottish votes, as Table 6.3 illustrates.

As may be seen, Labour is not nearly as dominant in its share of the Scottish votes as it is in its share of the Scottish seats. Any move towards an alternative electoral system would see Labour's share of the seats reduced. Added to this was the uncertainty of how the Scots

Table 6.3 Party distribution of Scottish votes 1970–9			
Party	1970	1974	1974	1979
Con	38.0	32.9	24.7	31.4
Lab	44.5	36.7	36.3	41.5
Lib	5.5	7.9	8.3	9.0
SNP	11.4	21.9	30.4	17.3

Source: http://www.psr.keele.ac.uk/psr.htm

would vote in elections for a devolved Parliament. Labour could find itself in a minority and losing control altogether. Hence the opposition by many in the Scottish Labour Party to the introduction of a different voting system for Scottish Parliament elections.

And yet this was what was eventually agreed between the two parties. The system would be a compromise however, of the additional member system; a hybrid which combined the simple plurality system and a regional party list. Many commentators have wondered why the Scottish Labour Party relented. In their book on devolved politics, Paterson, Brown, Curtice and Hinds suggest that the reason for the change of heart was perhaps that Labour eventually saw a proportional system as the main way of keeping the SNP out of power.[1]

If indeed this was the reason, then it was not particularly far-sighted given that within a decade, the SNP would indeed be in government in Scotland, with Labour, one of the architects of Scottish devolution, on the sidelines.

The landslide general election of May 1997 that brought Labour to power after eighteen years of opposition in Westminster also brought devolution back on to the political agenda. Unlike in the 1970s, when the issue could not be successfully implemented by the then minority Labour government, the Blair administration enjoyed a massive parliamentary majority. Moreover, the government acted quickly to get the process up and running. It produced a **White Paper** in July 1997 and planned a referendum for September 1997 (again not wanting to make the mistake of holding the referendum late in a Parliament, as in 1979).

This speed was facilitated by the fact that the government effectively had an off-the-peg system. The White Paper of July 1997 bore a close resemblance to 'Scotland's Parliament, Scotland's Right', published two years before. The aim was to see the first elections to the new Scottish Parliament held in May 1999. After the successful results of the referendum in September 1997, both parties which had, for different reasons, opposed devolution (the Conservatives and the SNP) pledged to respect the views of the Scottish people and work to make the new Parliament a successful political institution.

Voting in Scottish parliamentary elections

There have been three elections to the Scottish Parliament. As was mentioned in the case study in Chapter 4, the first two of these in 1999 and 2003 resulted in a **coalition** administration between Labour and the Liberal Democrats, while the third election in 2007 saw the SNP emerge as the party with the largest number of seats, although not a majority. The SNP went on to form a **minority government**.

A number of important questions need to be asked when analysing the outcomes of these elections. First, how do voting patterns compare between elections to the Scottish Parliament and elections of Scottish constituency MPs to Westminster? Secondly, are elections to the Scottish Parliament **second-order elections**, in other words are they treated less seriously than elections to the House of Commons? Which political parties have done well and less well out of the use of this electoral system? Does the additional member system itself affect the way in which Scotland's voters behave in elections to the Scottish Parliament?

Comparing Westminster and Holyrood elections

The results of the first elections in 1999 provide an interesting picture of the relative support for the main political parties compared with how they fared in the 1997 general election. Table 6.4 illustrates this.

As may be seen from Table 6.4, the Labour Party's share of the vote fell by nearly 7 per cent, mainly, it would appear, to the benefit

Table 6.4 Comparison of 1997 general election and 1999 Scottish Parliament election results

Party	1997 (%)	West-minster seats	1999 (first vote) %	1999 (second vote) %	SP seats
Labour	45.6	56	38.8	33.6	56
Conservative	17.5	0	15.6	15.4	18
Lib Dem	13.0	10	14.2	12.4	17
SNP	22.1	6	28.7	27.3	35

Source: R. Wyn Jones and R. Scully, 'Devolution and Electoral Politics in Scotland and Wales', *Publius: The Journal of Federalism*, vol. 36, no. 1, pp. 115–34, Oxford University Press.

of the Scottish National Party. In fact, Labour feared that the SNP would do better than it did. According to Richard Wyn Jones and Roger Scully, the result was a 'significant relief' to the Scottish Labour Party.[2] Indeed, members of the SNP had hoped that their party would break through the 30 per cent barrier.

Not illustrated in the table is the position of the small parties and independent candidates. Although they polled only 2.7 per cent of the **first vote** (the votes cast for constituency representatives), they polled 11.3 per cent of the **second vote** (the list votes).

The hopes by some nationalists that the first elections to the Scottish Parliament would result in the rise to power of the SNP were not borne out. What became clear, however, was the fact that the SNP was the main force of opposition in Scotland. This is a very important position to hold because in the mind of the electorate, this is effectively the alternative government, potentially one for the future.

The second elections to the Scottish Parliament were, however, not that future. They bore a resemblance to the election four years earlier insofar as the Labour Party remained the largest in terms of votes and seats. Table 6.5 illustrates the results in 2003 and compares them to the results of the 2001 general election.

Labour's share of the vote fell over 4 per cent compared to its

Table 6.5 Comparison of 2001 general election and 2003 Scottish Parliament election results

Party	2001 (%)	West-minster seats	First vote change from 1999 (%)	Second vote change from 1999 (%)	SP seats
Labour	43.3	55	34.5 (-4.4)	29.4 (-4.2)	50 (-6)
Conservative	15.6	1	16.6 (+1.0)	15.6 (+0.2)	18 (-)
Lib Dem	16.3	10	15.3 (+1.1)	11.8 (-0.6)	17 (-)
SNP	20.1	5	23.7 (-5.0)	20.9 (-6.5)	27 (-8)
Others	4.7	1	9.8 (+7.1)	22.2 (+10.9)	20 (+14)

Source: R. Wyn Jones and R. Scully, 'Devolution and Electoral Politics in Scotland and Wales', *Publius: The Journal of Federalism*, vol. 36, no. 1, pp. 115–34, Oxford University Press.

1999 figure and now the divergence on its Westminster result in 2001 was nearly 9 per cent. Perhaps the biggest story of the election was the fall in the share of the vote of the SNP, down 5 per cent on 1999. It is generally agreed that the party had not prospered under the leadership of John Swinney, who during the campaign was criticised by the press as being ineffective. Another suggestion is that the election took place shortly after the fall of Baghdad, in the early part of the war in Iraq. Both the SNP and the Liberal Democrats (whose vote also declined) had publicly opposed the military invasion.

The above tables may suggest that in the early years of devolution, UK-wide issues played as big a role as Scottish issues in elections to **Holyrood**. This, however, would assume that elections to the Scottish Parliament are second-order elections and Scottish voters do not distinguish between different elections. Indeed, if one looks at the shares of the vote achieved by the Conservatives, the Liberal Democrats and the SNP in 2003, the figures bear a close resemblance to their shares of the vote in 2001.

There is evidence, however, that disputes the idea that Scottish voters do not distinguish between elections to Westminster and to

Table 6.6 Hypothetical election to the Scottish Parliament 2001

Party	Westminster	Hypothetical Scottish Parliament vote (first vote)
Labour	43.3%	47.3%
Conservative	15.6%	9.6%
Lib Dem	16.3%	13.7%
SNP	20.1%	25.7%

Adapted from the 2001 Scottish Attitudes Survey.

Holyrood. Data collected for the Scottish Attitudes Survey illustrates this point, as Table 6.6 demonstrates.

This study asked voters in the 2001 general election how they would vote if there were to be a **hypothetical election** to the Scottish Parliament held at the same time. As may be seen, there is a divergence between how votes would be cast for different parties in different elections. The greatest of these is for the SNP, where it would appear that the party comes more into its own when the backdrop of the electoral battle is purely a Scottish one.

This analysis may be seen from the opposite direction by obtaining data from voters in the 2003 Scottish Parliament election being asked about their voting intentions in a hypothetical Westminster election. This data may be found in Table 6.7.

Once again there is a major divergence, although this time it is the Labour Party that sees the widest gap, followed by the SNP. Clearly, Scottish voters treat their votes in different ways. They appear capable of identifying the main issues that are important in these elections and using their vote accordingly. These figures would seem to suggest, therefore, that elections to the Scottish Parliament are not seen by voters as second-order elections, insofar as they are used as a protest vote against the party in government in Westminster.

The analysis so far has been confined to the first two elections to the Scottish Parliament. The following section looks at the outcome of the third election in 2007.

Table 6.7 Hypothetical general election 2003

Party	SP vote (first vote)	Hypothetical Westminster vote
Labour	35.7%	44.8%
Conservative	18.6%	19.8%
Lib Dem	13.4%	13.6%
SNP	25.5%	17.7%

Source: 2003 Scottish Attitudes Survey.

Box 6.1 The 2007 election to the Scottish Parliament

Table 6.8 provides data showing the relative performance of the political parties in the general election in 2005 and the 2007 election to the Scottish Parliament.

Table 6.8 Comparison of 2005 general election and 2007 Scottish Parliament election results

Party	2005 general election		2007 Scottish election	
	Votes	Seats	First votes	Seats
Conservative	15.8	1	16.6	17
Labour	38.9	40	32.1	46
Lib Dem	23.1	11	16.2	16
SNP	17.7	6	32.9	47

Source: BBC elections website.

There is clear evidence of a further decline in support for the Labour Party, a feature of the election across the whole of the United Kingdom. Given that Labour has traditionally seen Scotland as a stronghold, the results in 2005 must have been a portent of things to come in the next elections to the Scottish Parliament. Looking at the 2007 results, these fears were more than justified.

Care should be taken when analysing Labour's seats in 2005. This election was the first to be held with a reduced contingent of Scottish MPs in the House of Commons (down from seventy-two to fifty-nine). Labour was hit disproportionately by this reduction. Nevertheless, the previous analysis of Labour's fortune remains valid. Between the general elections of 2001 and 2005, Labour's share of the vote declined by over 4 per cent. This amounted to the loss of double the votes that Labour suffered between the general elections of 1997 and 2001.

Another interesting comparison between these two elections was the relative performance of the Liberal Democrats and the Scottish National Party. In 2005, the Liberal Democrats pushed the SNP into fourth place for the first time since the beginning of devolved government in Scotland. Yet within two years, the SNP's position had been transformed. This turnaround of fortunes adds significant weight to the argument that elections to the Scottish Parliament are not second-order elections. In other words, Scots were prepared to vote differently in an election where they believed that the SNP could make a real impact (Holyrood and not Westminster).

This election marked the end of the SNP's eight-year period of opposition in the Scottish Parliament. It also marked the end of an era of Labour dominance that had lasted over half a century. This was a truly historic result, not least because it was the first time that the SNP had beaten the Labour Party into second place in a nationwide election. It may be argued that the success of the SNP in 2007 was somewhat more difficult to explain than those of 1999 and 2003. Earlier in the chapter, it was suggested that in the case of the first two elections there was a clear Scottish dimension at work in the campaign rather than it being dominated by UK-wide issues. It may be argued that the outcome of the 2007 election was affected by wholly Scottish factors (such as positive impressions of the SNP mentioned earlier), as well as issues such as the Blair government's association with the war in Iraq (an issue that influenced voters across the UK).

Does this mean that by 2007, the Scottish elections were now being treated as second-order elections, with the voters expressing their views as a protest against the government in Westminster? Research conducted before the Scottish election in 2007 would appear to indicate otherwise. The public opinion organisation YouGov conducted a poll for *The Sunday Times* towards the end of the 2007 election campaign. The results seem to confirm what is illustrated in the above table. Voters appear to make a clear distinction between the two electoral arenas. Asked how they would vote in the next general election, 36 per cent of respondents said they would vote for Labour and 27 per cent for the SNP. In other words, compared with 2007, Labour will probably do better in Scotland at the next UK election and the SNP will do worse.

Throughout the period since the beginning of devolved government in Scotland, there has been clear evidence to suggest that Scottish voters do not treat elections to Holyrood as second-order ones. In this sense, the performance of a political party in these elections is not dependent upon what is happening in Westminster. These voters can identify particular institutions with specific issues and will vote accordingly.

For a fuller analysis of the outcome of the 2007 elections to the Scottish Parliament, see *Revolution or Evolution? The 2007 Scottish Elections*, by John Curtice, Michael Marsh, David McCrone, Nicola McEwen and Rachel Ormston (Edinburgh University Press, 2009).

The performance of political parties

The three elections to the Scottish Parliament have clearly reinforced the notion that Scotland has a four-party political system. This is not just to say that it is like the UK two-party system but with two other significant players; the whole order of party importance is different in Scotland. Currently the SNP and Labour occupy the top two places, with the Conservatives and Liberal Democrats vying with each other for third and fourth place.

The proportional nature of the voting system for elections to the Scottish Parliament has brought with it, as most observers and politicians thought it would, coalition government. This has created a new dynamic between the political parties. In Westminster politics, government has been an interplay between Labour and the Conservatives since 1922. In the first ten years in Scotland, however, three of the four main parties have played a part in governing the country. Indeed, following the 2007 Scottish election, it was briefly thought that a fifth party, the Greens, might form a coalition with the Scottish National Party.

The Scottish National Party

The biggest winner in Scotland has clearly been the SNP. Although a force in the country for nearly forty years, the most the party had been able to show for it was a small rump of MPs in the House of Commons. Devolution could in many ways be seen as a 'home game' for the SNP. The debates and controversies in elections to Holyrood are dedicated territory for the party. All of the other main political parties may be seen to be forces from south of the border.

The proportional voting system propelled the SNP into the role of official opposition in the first elections in 1999 and from this position it was only a matter of time until it would get its chance to be in government. Paradoxically, the proportional electoral system probably prevented the party from becoming a majority government and in 2007 it failed to woo another party into coalition government. The SNP formed a minority government, which gives a majority of seats in the Scottish Parliament to all the other parties combined.

The SNP gambled on the notion that the other parties would not combine to bring down their administration, at least in the first few years, because none really appeared to have the stomach (or in the case of Labour, the money) to fight another election. This calculation nearly went awry in early 2009, however, when the SNP had its **budget** blocked by MSPs. It was only after long negotiations between the political parties that a revised budget was passed. Another storm appeared to be gathering around the SNP administration after it released the man convicted of the Lockerbie bombing in August 2009.

The Liberal Democrats

In terms of votes the Liberal Democrats have not done any better in Scottish parliamentary elections than in elections to the House of Commons. The tables earlier in this chapter show that at best the party has polled 1 to 2 per cent extra in elections to the Scottish Parliament. The real story here is what these votes have enabled the party to achieve.

The Liberal Democrats have been fighting for proportional representation for decades. With the introduction of elections to Holyrood, there has been the opportunity for the party to take a part in coalition government. Given the closeness that existed between the

Liberal Democrats and the Labour Party in Scotland in the 1990s, it seemed only natural that having failed to secure a majority in its own right in 1999, Labour would form a coalition with the Liberal Democrats.

Despite sharing government with Labour between 1999 and 2007, the Liberal Democrats did not suffer the same decline in support as Labour did in the 2007 elections. This poses an interesting question. Why should one party in a coalition fare worse than another? It could be that, as the dominant party in the coalition, Labour was bound to take most of the blame for mistakes that were made. There is, of course, another explanation. Perhaps it was the performance of the Labour Party outside Scotland that was really the subject of voters' disapproval in 2007. If this was the case, the debate about whether these are second-order elections remains unsettled.

The Conservative Party

The story for the Conservative Party in Scotland over the past fifty years has been one of decline. By the 1990s it was down to a single Scottish seat in the House of Commons and in 1997 that seat was lost. From a parliamentary perspective, therefore, at the time of the referendum later in the same year, Scotland was a Conservative-free zone. The Conservatives campaigned hard against devolution as a matter of high principle, despite the knowledge that this stance was one of the reasons for the party's unpopularity in Scotland.

Scotland was not and is not a Conservative-free zone, however, although its level of support has seriously declined. In 1955, the party took 51 per cent of Scottish votes (beating the Labour Party on 48 per cent). By 1992, that figure had fallen to just 24 per cent.[3]

By 1997 the figure had fallen to 17.5 per cent (see the table above). While this figure is a shadow of what it once was, it still represents a significant slice of the Scottish vote. Nearly a fifth of Scottish voters supported the Conservatives in 1997 and did not see a single Conservative returned to the House of Commons.

There is something of a paradox here. The Conservatives have long argued against electoral as well as constitutional reform. Their preferred simple plurality system, which had helped them and Labour to hold on to alternating periods of government, was hurting them north of the border. Even faced with this, the Conservatives argued against devolution and against the use of a proportional voting system to elect it. Ten years later and the Conservatives do have a voice in Scotland and a presence in the Scottish Parliament that their share of the vote warrants.

The Labour Party
The Labour Party is the big loser in Scotland. The first decade of devolution has seen its position significantly worsen and is a far cry from its hegemony in the country over a period of fifty years. This has coincided with a weakening of support for Labour in Scotland in elections to the House of Commons.

This decline in support has two dimensions in Scotland. In the first place there is the loss of votes that has taken place over this period. This shows that the party's share of the vote has declined from just under 40 per cent in 1999 to just over 32 per cent in 2007. It is perhaps too early to declare whether this is part of a longer-term trend or just the normal ebb and flow of politics, albeit a rather long ebb. Whatever the case, it represents a blow to the party that dominated Scotland for so long and made it possible for the country to have its first Parliament for nearly 300 years.

Secondly, and perhaps more importantly, with a proportional voting system, this loss of votes has impacted on the party's capacity to govern. When agreeing to a proportional voting system, members of the Scottish Labour Party recognised that coalitions would be likely and that it was feasible that one day it might find itself outside government. The loss of power to the SNP after only eight years of devolved government represents a further and bitter blow to the party.

For a useful history of devolution in Scotland, see *Uncharted Territory: The Story of Scottish Devolution 1999–2009* by Hamish Macdonell (Politico's Publishing, 2009).

The impact of the additional member system

Clearly, the use of a proportional voting system did have an effect on the outcome of the elections to the Scottish Parliament. In all three elections, no party secured a majority of seats and therefore the final outcome was either a coalition (1999 and 2001) or a minority administration (2007).

It has been suggested that in 2007, the system itself and the way that it was operated could have made a significant difference to the outcome of the election. The electoral authorities redesigned ballot papers to make more room for the list candidates. In so doing the amount of space devoted to voting instructions was reduced and it has been suggested that this led to an increase in the number of **spoilt ballot papers**. Robert Johns, Christopher Carman and David Denver indicate that 'more than one in five (16 of the 72) constituencies were won by a smaller margin than the number of rejected votes recorded'.[4]

Christopher Carman, James Mitchell and Robert Johns argue that this problem was particularly acute in Lothians and Glasgow, where the high levels of **social deprivation** and low levels of education contributed to the higher number of spoilt ballot papers this time round.[5]

Given that the 2007 election was very close, such high rates of rejected ballots were more of an issue than they would have been had the election been more clear cut. In 2007, there was only a one-seat difference between Labour and the SNP and fewer than fifty votes between the two parties in the most closely fought constituency.

The above points reflect the way that the operation of the process and design of the ballot paper might have contributed to the result. Up until 2007, however, there was no ready way of comparing the impact of the additional member system to a different proportional electoral system. That year saw the introduction of the single transferable vote in elections for Scottish local councils. Table 6.9 shows the difference between votes for the parties in both parliamentary and council elections in 2007.

Given that these elections took place on the same day, it is interesting to compare the figures. It suggests a differential support for all the main political parties, albeit a minor one. Perhaps at the margins, in a closely run contest, the precise nature of the electoral system can make a difference to the outcome of the election. In this case the figures would appear to indicate that Labour would have done slightly better using the single transferable vote and because of the narrow margin in 2007, this might have been enough to enable it to hold on to power in the Scottish Parliament.

Table 6.9 Comparison of 2007 Scottish Parliament election and local council elections results

Party	Scottish Parliament (vote)	Local council (vote)
Conservative	16.6	18.5
Labour	32.1	33.4
Lib Dem	16.2	15.1
SNP	32.9	33.0

What you should have learnt from reading this chapter

- An understanding of the background and recent history of voting behaviour in Scotland

- A knowledge of the background to devolution in Scotland

- The results of the three elections to the Scottish Parliament

- An evaluation of elections to the Scottish Parliament and to Westminster

- The fortunes of the political parties in elections to the Scottish Parliament

- The use of the additional member system

 ## Glossary of key terms

Budget The Scottish Executive works within a budget in order to provide services to the people of Scotland. Each year, this budget is presented for the approval of the Scottish Parliament, which decides whether to approve the budget or not. With a majority in the Parliament, there should be no difficulty in getting the budget passed. Without a majority, the minority governing party is at the mercy of the other political parties with seats in the Scottish Parliament

Coalition A partnership of two or more political parties in government. This normally occurs when a single political party falls short of a parliamentary majority to form a government on its own. This is not the norm in British politics. In countries operating proportional voting systems, however, they are quite common.

First vote In the additional member system, voters cast two votes. The first vote is the one cast in a constituency using the simple plurality method of voting.

Holyrood This is the place in Edinburgh where the Scottish Parliament is situated. The two terms are interchangeable – rather like referring to the UK Parliament as Westminster.

Hypothetical election This is not a real election. Public opinion bodies often ask the question, 'If there were a general election held tomorrow, which party would you support?' The studies cited in this chapter asked voters who had participated in elections to the Scottish Parliament to declare how they would have voted if there had been a general election held at the same time.

Minority government When a party seeks to govern without a majority of seats and does not enter into a coalition with another party. In such circumstances, the government is vulnerable to defeat in votes in the House of Commons. Between February and October 1974, and between 1976 and 1979, Britain had a minority Labour government.

Second-order elections A term used to describe elections where voters might choose to use a protest vote against the government in Westminster. Local council elections or elections to the European Parliament are often described as such. If voters are seen to vote in a devolved election on the basis of devolved rather than UK-wide issues and differently to the way they would in a general election, then the elections concerned would not be described as second-order elections.

Second vote In the additional member system, voters cast two votes. The second vote is based on the party list proportional system with the voter casting a vote for the party and not for an individual candidate.

Social deprivation This is a term used to describe poor socio-economic conditions. Some of the UK's biggest towns have areas which are socially deprived, with income levels usually well below the UK median, poor housing conditions and a high level of unemployment.

Spoilt ballot papers Most ballot papers contain a set of instructions on how to cast a vote. In the simple plurality system the process is fairly straightforward: an instruction to place a cross next to the preferred candidate. Other electoral systems are often more complicated and require more elaborate instructions. If a voter fails to follow the instructions by, for example, voting for more candidates than allowed, then the ballot paper will be deemed 'spoilt' and will not be counted.

White Paper A document which the government publishes just before it goes ahead with a piece of legislation. It is the final time the proposals can be considered more widely before the debate becomes confined to the House of Commons and the House of Lords.

? Likely examination questions

Distinguish between the outcomes of the three elections to the Scottish Parliament.

'Devolution has made no real difference to political parties in Scotland.' Discuss.

Helpful websites

Scottish Parliament website

http://www.scottish.parliament.uk/

Scottish Electoral Commission

http://www.electoralcommission.org.uk/scotland

Vote Scotland website

http://www.votescotland.com/stv/CCC_FirstPage.jsp

ASPECT (Access to Scottish Parliamentary Election Candidate Materials)

http://gdl.cdlr.strath.ac.uk/aspect/

Scottish Election Study

http://www.scottishelectionstudy.org.uk/

Suggestions for further reading

C. Carmen, J. Mitchell and R. Johns, 'The unfortunate natural experiment in ballot design: the Scottish Parliamentary Elections of 2007', *Electoral Studies*, vol. 27, no. 3, pp. 442–59, 2008.

P. Norris, *Electoral Change since 1945*, Blackwell, 1997.

L. Paterson, A. Brown, J. Curtice and K. Hinds, *New Scotland, New Politics*, Edinburgh University Press, 2002.

R. Wyn Jones and R. Scully, 'Devolution and Electoral Politics in Scotland and Wales', *Publius: The Journal of Federalism*, vol. 36, no. 1, pp. 115–34, 2006.

CHAPTER 7

Voting in Wales

Contents

Overview

The Blair government held a referendum on Welsh devolution in 1997, the result of which means that Wales has elected its own Assembly since 1999. As part of the new constitutional arrangements in Wales, the new Assembly has been elected using a different electoral system from that used by Welsh voters to elect MPs to the House of Commons.

This chapter explores the differences between voting in Wales in general elections and in those for the devolved Assembly. In addition, there will be an examination of the fortunes of the main political parties in Wales. Finally, there will be an assessment of how the additional member system of voting has affected the outcome of the devolved elections in Wales.

Key issues to be covered in this chapter

- The background of voting behaviour in Wales
- The distinction between Welsh Assembly and Westminster elections
- How the main political parties have fared in devolved elections in Wales
- The additional member electoral system in Wales

Background

As in Scotland, the political system in Wales has been dominated by the Labour Party. Unlike in Scotland, this dominance has been entrenched not merely for the last fifty years but for nearly a century. Indeed, Wales has been seen by many political commentators as the bedrock of Labour's support in the whole of the United Kingdom.

The Conservative Party has traditionally fared very poorly in Welsh (Westminster) parliamentary constituencies. The Liberal Party was, up until a century ago, the major force in Wales and its successors, the Liberal Democrats, retain a number of Welsh seats in Westminster, particularly in rural border areas.

The political situation in Wales is a more complicated one than perhaps so far described. There is something of a north-south, rural-urban divide in Welsh voting patterns. The latter may not come as a huge surprise. In Chapter 5, voting patterns in the UK as a whole were shown to have had a rural-urban divide about them. As with the rest of the UK, Labour tends to do better in towns than in the country. What is different is that the rural areas are not dominated by the Conservatives but by other parties such as the Liberal Democrats and **Plaid Cymru** (the Welsh nationalists). The **north–south divide** is the opposite of that observed in England. In Wales, Labour has been traditionally strongest in the south of the country. It is in these constituencies that most of Welsh heavy industry such as coal mining and steel making were located. In the north, Plaid Cymru has prospered to a greater extent.

As in Scotland, the forces of nationalism in Wales began to make big strides in the 1960s. Some spectacular by-election wins from 1966 onwards meant that the Labour government of Harold Wilson had to sit up and take note of what was happening in one of its major bastions of electoral support. How do the nationalist causes in Scotland and Wales compare?

There are two main ways in which these two movements may be contrasted. In the first instance, there is the issue of scale. Plaid Cymru was never able to match the level of support among Welsh voters that the SNP achieved in Scotland in the 1970s. Secondly, the nature of Welsh nationalism differed markedly from that in Scotland. The SNP based its bid for independence on a rationalist model that the country had the economic means to support itself, particularly with the advent of North Sea oil revenues in the 1970s ('Scotland's Oil', as the SNP slogans of the time proclaimed). In Wales, there was a greater cultural focus and a particular stress on the maintenance and promotion of the Welsh language. Indeed, for a period in the 1990s, Plaid Cymru actually dropped its commitment to a fully independent Wales.

These asymmetries are the main reason for the different ways that Labour in the 1970s and again in the 1990s attempted to deal with devolution in Scotland and in Wales. On both occasions Scotland was to be given a 'Parliament' and Wales was to be offered an 'Assembly'. Today the Scottish Parliament enjoys **legislative devolution**, in that it can pass laws, **financial devolution**, in that it can vary the rate of income tax, as well as **administrative devolution**, in that it can run services such as education and health. Wales enjoys only administrative devolved powers.

The extent of the difference between Scottish and Welsh support for the nationalist cause is illustrated in Figure 7.1.

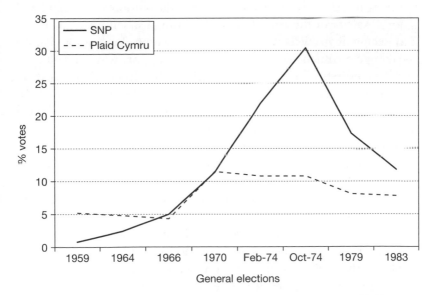

Source: Table created using data from UK Election Statistics: 1945–2000, House of Commons Library Research Paper 01/37.

Figure 7.1 Nationalist support in Scotland and Wales in general elections 1959–83

As may be seen, nationalist support peaked in Wales before it did in Scotland. After 1970, support for Plaid Cymru stopped increasing and started to tail off. In Scotland, the SNP hit a sharp peak in 1974 before falling quickly in the 1980s. The really significant feature of this chart, however, is the magnitude of nationalist support in the two countries. In the years following the Second World War, Plaid Cymru made the greater impact in electoral terms. The SNP had a third of the Scottish vote in October 1974, nearly three times what Plaid Cymru achieved at its peak in 1970.

It could be argued that the nationalist threat in Wales was not as serious to Labour as it was in Scotland, as nationalist support in Wales was less than in Scotland. In addition, there were fewer parliamentary constituencies in Wales than in Scotland. These factors combined meant that there was much less propensity for Plaid Cymru to damage Labour in Wales compared with the electoral damage that the SNP was able to inflict upon the Labour Party in Scotland.

The combined influence of the two nationalist movements could not be ignored, however. To have offered devolution to Scotland and ignore Wales ran the risk of fuelling nationalist sentiment in Wales and seeing it grow beyond the five or six predominantly Welsh-speaking constituencies where most of its support was concentrated and into more traditional Labour territory. It is interesting that Plaid Cymru has indeed seen its support grow beyond its natural constituency; ironically this has come about not because Wales was denied devolution but as a consequence of being given it.

Welsh devolution has proven to be more problematic for the Labour Party. The Welsh voted decisively against it in the referendum in 1979. Nationalists argued that this was because the proposals on offer were inadequate and that there would have been a more positive response to more ambitious devolution plans for Wales. There are a number of problems with this analysis, however, not least of which can be seen in the chart above. If the nationalists were right and the Welsh wanted a devolved assembly with more powers, one might have expected a rise in support for Plaid Cymru in the general election that took place two months after the referendum. In fact, nationalist support fell in the 1979 general election, hardly a resounding result for the cause of more Welsh autonomy.

The referendum in 1997 proved that the Welsh had warmed to

the idea of devolution. The result was very close, however, with the 'Yes' campaign only narrowly beating the 'No' campaign. The result was a far cry from the one in Scotland where, one week earlier, over 70 per cent had voted for a devolved Parliament and over 60 per cent voted to give it tax-varying powers.

The first elections for the new National Assembly for Wales would be held on the same day as those for the Scottish Parliament. The same proportional electoral system would be employed, that is, the additional member voting system. Given that the nationalist challenge was more limited in Wales than in Scotland, Labour was more sanguine about the use of a proportional electoral system to elect the National Assembly for Wales. Indeed, in normal times, the Labour Party would have been confident that it would not need to resort to coalition governments in Wales, given how dominant the party was there. As will be seen, however, the circumstances of the 1999 election for the National Assembly for Wales proved that these were not 'normal times'.

Voting in Welsh Assembly elections

There have been three elections to the National Assembly for Wales, and none of them resulted in an Assembly majority for the Labour Party. In the first two of these, in 1999 and 2003, Labour became the governing party but, without a majority of Assembly seats, these were effectively **minority governments** (although there was a brief pact between Labour and the Liberal Democrats between 1999 and 2000). The most recent Assembly election in 2007 saw Labour and Plaid Cymru forming a **coalition** administration.

As in the previous chapter, a number of key questions need to be asked when analysing the outcomes of these elections. First, how do voting patterns compare between elections to the National Assembly for Wales and elections of Welsh constituency MPs to Westminster? Secondly, are elections to the National Assembly for Wales **second-order elections**, in other words are they treated less seriously than elections to the House of Commons? Which political parties have done well and less well out of the use of this electoral system? Does the additional member system itself affect the way in which the voters of Wales behave in elections to the National Assembly for Wales?

Table 7.1 Comparison of 1997 general election and 1999 Welsh Assembly election results

Party	1997 (%)	West-minster seats	1999 (first vote) %	1999 (second vote) %	NAW seats
Labour	54.8	34	37.6	35.5	28
Conservative	19.5	0	15.8	16.5	9
Lib Dem	12.3	2	13.5	12.6	6
Plaid Cymru	10.0	4	28.4	30.6	17

Source: R. Wyn Jones and R. Scully, 'Devolution and Electoral Politics in Scotland and Wales', Publius: The Journal of Federalism, vol. 36, no. 1, pp. 115–34, Oxford University Press.

Comparing Westminster and Cardiff elections

The results of the first elections in 1999 provide an interesting picture of the relative support for the main political parties compared with how they fared in the 1997 general election. Table 7.1 illustrates this.

Compared with a similar table in the previous chapter, comparing the outcome of the 1997 general election with that of the first elections to the Scottish Parliament, the results in Wales are remarkable. They show a dramatic drop in the share of the Labour vote of almost 17 per cent. The figures show an equally impressive increase in support for Plaid Cymru. In both Scotland and in Wales, it became clear that in the devolved bodies, it would be the nationalist parties that would be the main forces of opposition.

The scale of Labour's decline might not be seen solely in the light of the popularity of Plaid Cymru, however. One big factor in explaining Labour's relatively poor showing was the infighting that had gone on at the top of the Welsh Labour Party, leaving many in Wales feeling that despite devolution, the New Labour machine in London was trying to impose its preferred choice to lead the party in Wales. If this was true, then these results might just be a peculiarity. Only the results of future elections would determine whether this was in fact the case.

Table 7.2 Comparison of 2001 general election and 2003 Welsh Assembly election results

Party	2001 (%)	West-minster seats	First vote change from 1999 (%)	Second vote change from 1999 (%)	NAW seats
Labour	48.6	34	40.0 (+2.4)	36.6 (+1.1)	30 (+2)
Conservative	21.0	0	19.9 (+4.0)	19.2 (+3.2)	11 (+2)
Lib Dem	13.8	3	14.1 (+0.6)	12.7 (+0.1)	6 (-)
Plaid Cymru	14.3	4	21.2 (-7.2)	19.7 (-10.8)	12(-5)
Others	2.3	0	4.8 (+0.1)	11.8 (+6.9)	1 (+1)

Source: R. Wyn Jones and R. Scully, 'Devolution and Electoral Politics in Scotland and Wales', *Publius: The Journal of Federalism*, vol. 36, no. 1, pp. 115–34, Oxford University Press.

The second elections took place four years later, in 2003. Table 7.2 offers the results of these elections and the results of the 2001 general election in Wales.

As can be seen from the table, Labour did recover somewhat at the expense of Plaid Cymru. An interesting parallel between these results and those in Scotland was the issue of leadership. In the previous chapter, the impact of a new leader for the SNP was discussed. Plaid Cymru also saw a change of leader in 2003, with the retirement of the popular figure Ieuan Wyn Jones. This may also account for some of the fall in nationalist support in Wales that same year. Many commentators observing the results in 2003 believed that the tide of nationalist support in Wales was ebbing.

The result, however, still meant that Labour was one seat short of a majority in the Welsh Assembly and in spite of the recovery from 1999, the party was still over 8 per cent below its performance in the general election of 2001. Labour's recovery, therefore, may be seen as a fragile one.

At this point, some mention should be made of minor parties. One of the arguments for adopting a proportional election system

Table 7.3 Hypothetical general election 1999

Party	NAW vote (first vote)	Hypothetical Westminster vote
Labour	37.5%	53.3%
Conservative	14.0%	18.4%
Lib Dem	12.4%	11.6%
Plaid Cymru	30.8%	14.9%

Source: 1999 Welsh National Assembly Election Study.

is to enable fairer representation for all parties, including those that normally fail to be represented at all. In spite of receiving over 10 per cent of the regional (additional or second) votes, only one of these candidates gained a seat in the National Assembly for Wales in the election of 2003. In this sense, smaller political parties were not helped that much by the additional member system in the way that it operated in these Assembly elections.

An important question to ask at this point is regarding the salience of UK-wide issues in the campaigns and outcomes of elections to the National Assembly for Wales. Do Welsh voters vote in Assembly elections on Welsh issues or do they use them as an opportunity to register a protest vote against the government in Westminster? The answer to these questions should indicate whether elections to the National Assembly for Wales are second-order elections.

As in the case of Scotland, research has been carried out to compare voting intentions between elections for Welsh seats in the House of Commons and in elections to the National Assembly for Wales. Table 7.3 offers an illustration.

This study asked voters in the 1999 Assembly election how they would vote if there were to be a **hypothetical election** (that is, a general election) held at the same time. As may be seen, there are a number of clear divergences between how votes would be cast for different parties in different types of election. The greatest disparity is in the support for Labour and Plaid Cymru. A general election would have boosted Labour's share of the vote by over 15 per cent.

Table 7.4 Hypothetical election to the Welsh Assembly 2001

Party	Westminster	Hypothetical NAW vote (first vote)
Labour	48.6%	49.4%
Conservative	21.0%	10.6%
Lib Dem	13.8%	11.9%
Plaid Cymru	14.3%	26.2%

Adapted from the 2001 Wales Life and Times Survey.

In contrast to this, Plaid Cymru's support would more than halve in the event of a general election.

This analysis may be seen from the opposite direction, as shown in Table 7.4, which compares the actual general election result in Wales in 2001 with a hypothetical election to the National Assembly for Wales.

This data appears to be far less dramatic. Labour would appear to fare only marginally worse in a hypothetical election to the National Assembly for Wales compared to the result in Wales in the 2001 general election. The divergence for Plaid Cymru remains wide; their vote would almost double if it were an Assembly election rather than a general election. As in the case of Scotland, discussed in Chapter 6, it would appear that the nationalist party in Wales is fighting elections to the Assembly on a much firmer footing.

It is as clear in Wales as it is in Scotland that voters treat their votes in different ways. They appear capable of identifying the main issues that are important in these elections and using their vote accordingly. These figures would seem to suggest, therefore, that elections to the National Assembly for Wales are not seen by voters as second-order elections, insofar as they are used as a protest vote against the party in government in Westminster.

The analysis so far has been confined to the first two elections to the National Assembly for Wales. The following section looks at the outcome of the third election, in 2007.

Box 7.1 The 2007 election to the National Assembly for Wales

The Electoral Commission has produced a detailed analysis of the 2007 elections to the National Assembly for Wales.[1] Table 7.5 provides data showing the relative performance of the political parties in the general election in 2005 and the 2007 election to the National Assembly for Wales.

Table 7.5 Comparison of 2005 general election and 2007 Welsh Assembly election results

Party	2005 general election		2007 Welsh election	
	Votes	Seats	First votes	Seats
Conservative	21.4	3	22.4	12
Labour	42.7	29	32.2	26
Lib Dem	18.4	4	14.8	6
Plaid Cymru	12.6	3	22.4	15
Others	5.0	1	8.3	1

Sources: Table created using data from UK Election Statistics 1918–2007, House of Commons Library Research Paper 08/12, National Assembly for Wales, 2007 Assembly Election Results.

Both elections saw Labour's share of the vote fall. In the case of the 2005 general election, this contributed (albeit marginally) to the reduction of Labour's overall majority in the House of Commons, but still left the party in government. In the case of the 2007 election to the National Assembly for Wales, the decline in support was to have a more dramatic effect. After a brief coalition with the Liberal Democrats between 1999 and 2000, Labour served on government alone up until 2003, continuing in office with thirty of the sixty Assembly seats until 2007. In 2007, Labour lost four seats and was five seats short of an overall Assembly majority. It remained the largest party, however, so there was little chance of it being forced into opposition (unless Plaid Cymru, the Conservatives and the Liberal Democrats were willing to share power in a coalition, which seemed unlikely). In the event, Labour and Plaid Cymru went into coalition with each other. John Osmond's publication for the Institute of Welsh Affairs provides a useful analysis of the latest developments in politics in Wales.[2]

The 2005 general election saw an increase in Conservative support with the party winning three seats (its first constituency wins to the House of Commons since 1997). It is interesting to note that the Conservatives in Wales might be the unlikely beneficiaries of devolution. The proportional system used to elect Assembly members effectively put the Conservatives on the political map. To what extent has this presence enhanced the salience of the Conservatives to the extent that more voters are willing to vote for the party in a general election as well?

As in the case of the 2007 election to the Scottish Parliament, the Welsh result marked an important step in the history of Plaid Cymru. The outcome of the election gave the nationalists their first taste of political power in Wales. Unlike the result in Scotland, however, the nationalists were unable to relegate the Labour Party into second place. This perhaps is explained by the point made earlier in this chapter about the differences between nationalist support in Scotland and in Wales. In Scotland the SNP has been able to attract votes from regions across the country and reach levels of support that make the party a real contender for political power. In Wales, nationalist strength is somewhat more geographically confined, as the following map of the 2007 results for the National Assembly for Wales confirms.

Although Plaid Cymru did manage to take seats from Labour in places such as Llanelli, its support is largely confined to central and northern Wales. The party failed to make any inroads into the urban Labour heartlands of the valleys in south Wales. This perhaps implies that the appeal of nationalism in Wales is more limited than it is in Scotland. The outcome of this election did not see Labour losing power. It did, however, see Plaid Cymru taking a share of political power in Wales, something that many commentators would have considered unthinkable a decade before.

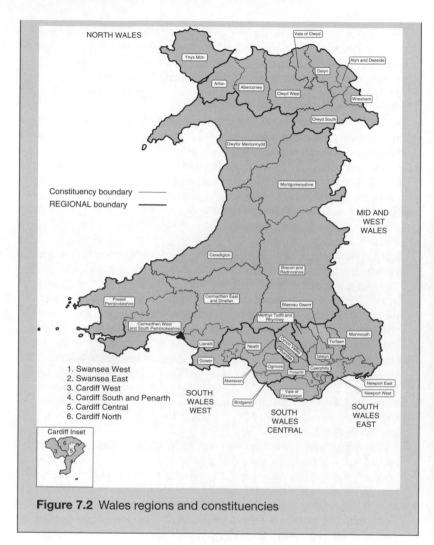

Figure 7.2 Wales regions and constituencies

The performance of political parties

As in Scotland, the three elections to the National Assembly for Wales have demonstrated that Wales is a four-party political system, albeit an unequal one. The 1999 result showed a 'big two–little two' split in the way that support for the four parties divided; Labour and Plaid Cymru being the 'big two', the Conservatives and the Liberal

Democrats being the 'little two'. By 2003, however, the dynamic had altered somewhat. Labour had moved into a more dominant position, with the Conservatives and Plaid Cymru well behind with similar percentages of the vote. The Liberal Democrats fell behind these latter two parties. These positions were replicated in the 2007 Assembly election, with the gap between front-running Labour and the Conservatives and Plaid Cymru being much narrower. This would appear to suggest that support for three of the four main political parties in Wales is somewhat fluid and subject to change. This is not to suggest that the Conservatives will form the next administration in Wales, rather that Labour can no longer take for granted being able to dominate the Welsh political system. Indeed, the coalition government that resulted from the 2007 elections to the National Assembly for Wales bears this point out very well.

Unlike in Scotland, coalition government was not anticipated by any of the political parties early on in the history of devolved politics in Wales. As time has progressed, however, a combination of factors, including, of course, the workings of the additional member voting system, have created a political environment conducive to coalition government. These are still early days, however, and it is not unfeasible that a single party will be able to garner sufficient support in the future to be able to form a single-party government.

Indeed, it is interesting to note that after eight years of single-party (albeit minority) government in Wales between 1999 and 2007, a coalition government came about when exactly the opposite was happening in Scotland. There, nearly eight years of coalition government was supplanted in 2007 by a single-party (the SNP) minority government.

Plaid Cymru

Plaid Cymru has long been seen as a less significant player in Welsh politics than the SNP in Scotland. Earlier in this chapter it was explained that the scale of Welsh nationalism was more limited than its counterpart in Scotland. Plaid Cymru never reached across the regions as well as the Scottish National Party and it never achieved electoral support in elections to the House of Commons.

This was often put down to the message of Plaid Cymru, which, it was suggested, concentrated on cultural and linguistic concerns, which were confined to certain parts of central and north Wales. These matters failed to resonate with the majority of Welsh electors in the south of the country, who maintained their loyalty to the Labour Party long after class and partisan dealignment were eroding its support in much of England.

The scale of the success of the SNP in Scotland was not, therefore, unexpected. The initial performance of Plaid Cymru in 1999 was much more of a surprise. Much of this can be attributed to difficulties being experienced within the Welsh Labour Party at the time and Plaid Cymru's support has fallen back since then. However, the party remains well ahead of the level of support it achieved in any previous general elections. In the 2007 elections to the National Assembly for Wales, support was 12 per cent higher than the figure the party achieved in the 1997 general election.

As mentioned previously, some commentators were ready to write off the party after the 2001 Assembly elections by stating that its support was ebbing. The 2007 Assembly result showed that that was not the case and that as well as holding on to its share of the vote, it also had a share in political power in Wales. In the previous chapter, it was argued that the Scottish National Party was the real winner of the introduction of devolution. It would seem that Plaid Cymru also has plenty to be hopeful about when it looks to the future of devolution in Wales.

The electoral success of Plaid Cymru and the somewhat dynamic nature of Welsh politics since the introduction of devolution have seen increased support for devolution in the country. Indeed, the National Assembly for Wales commissioned Lord Richard, a Labour peer in the House of Lords, to investigate the ways that the powers of the Assembly could be enhanced. His report, published in 2004, made a number of proposals, including changing the voting system for Assembly elections to the single transferable vote.

The Liberal Democrats

If there is a real contrast to be drawn between Scottish and Welsh devolution, the story is to be found in the fortunes of the Liberal Democrats. At first sight there would appear to be some similarity between the fortunes of the party in elections to the Scottish Parliament and the National Assembly for Wales. In both countries the party's percentage share of the vote has been in the mid teens (in Scotland a range between 14.2 per cent and 16.2 per cent; in Wales a range between 13.5 per cent and 14.8 per cent). In terms of seats, the Liberal Democrats have had 10 per cent of the seats in all three elections to the National Assembly for Wales. In Scotland the figure has been slightly higher at around 13 per cent.

The Liberal Democrats have not really profited from devolution in Wales. In the first instance, the party's share of the vote in elections to the National Assembly for Wales is only marginally higher than it was in Welsh elections to the House of Commons and well behind its UK average percentage vote. Perhaps more significantly, the Liberal Democrats were unable to take a share in political power as they had been able to in Scotland.

Indeed, after years of single-party government, when the time did come for a coalition of parties in Wales, it was the nationalists that the Labour Party turned to rather than the Liberal Democrats. One of the reasons for this might have been the failure of the Labour–Liberal Democrat pact that endured only between 1999 and 2000. In a four- party system, the Liberal Democrats have had to come to terms with the fact that they are not the only party capable of playing the power broking card. The fact that this role came more naturally to them in Scotland may say more about the different relationships that exist between the main political parties there. In Wales, it seems that Labour was prepared to deal with the nationalists, which in Scotland would have been almost unthinkable at the time. Perhaps also relations between Labour and the Liberal Democrats have been closer in Scotland than between their counterparts in Wales.

The Conservative Party

The Conservatives have long been regarded in Wales in a similar vein to the Conservatives in Scotland, as a virtual electoral irrelevance. The main difference, however, is that at one time, the Conservatives were a major political force in Scotland. The same cannot be said of the party in Wales. By the 1990s this historical difference was somewhat irrelevant because the party had been effectively wiped out in terms of Scottish and Welsh Westminster constituency seats.

As with Scotland, however, the level of the Conservative Party's support in Wales cannot be measured by the number of House of Commons seats it wins. In Wales, the Conservative level of support was about 20 per cent in these elections (a figure marginally greater than their showing in Scotland). Conservative supporters were being denied proper representation. In spite of this, the Conservatives opposed Labour's devolution proposals for Wales in 1997, even though they would pave the way for a Conservative presence in the new Welsh Assembly.

In terms of votes, the Conservatives have fared slightly worse in elections to the National Assembly for Wales than in the Welsh constituencies to the House of Commons. However, the use of the additional member system for devolved elections in Wales means that the party gains seats where it does not in Westminster, where the elections are fought using the simple plurality system. The Conservatives are not presently serious contenders for political power in Wales, but the voting system at least enables those Welsh people with Conservative leanings to be represented for the first time at a national level.

In the 2005 general election, mentioned earlier in this chapter, although the Conservatives lost a third consecutive time to Labour, they did make a number of parliamentary gains; this included three House of Commons seats from Welsh constituencies. This represented something of an advance in Wales for the Conservatives. Perhaps the National Assembly for Wales, the institution that the party was opposed to creating in 1997, has acted to seed the idea of voting Conservative to larger numbers of Welsh voters when general elections come round. Indeed the Conservatives made further advances in Wales in the 2010 general election (gaining five seats).

The Labour Party

The Labour Party has experienced mixed fortunes in Wales since the first devolved elections in 1999. The first set of results was a clear blow to the party, representing as it did a major fall on its share of the vote in the general election two years before. The party made a slight recovery in 2001 (a 2.4 per cent increase on 1999). This increase also enabled the party to secure an additional two seats in the National Assembly for Wales, which effectively made the Labour administration more secure in its second term than it had been in its first.

The percentage figure that the party achieved in 2001 was still nearly 9 per cent less than it had achieved in Welsh constituencies in the 2001 general election. By the 2007 Assembly elections, Labour's support had slumped to an even lower figure than in 1999. By the third election to the National Assembly for Wales, Labour could count on fewer than one in three Welsh votes. This represents a major decline of a party that was until recently a towering force in Wales.

As in Scotland, therefore, Labour seems to have been the loser, at least in the longer term. History tells us that even with a proportional voting system, Labour should have dominated the Welsh devolved government. As it is, it clung to power in a minority administration for seven years before finally being forced to join forces with the nationalists in a coalition government after the results of the 2007 Assembly elections were declared.

It could be argued that, as in Scotland, the Labour Party had everything to lose from devolved government. The salience of Scottish and Welsh issues has clearly helped the nationalist movements in both countries. The use of the additional member electoral system has worked to prevent a single political party from governing with a majority. Perhaps, however, history will judge that it was in Wales that Labour's fall was greatest.

The impact of the additional member system

Clearly, the use of a proportional voting system did have an effect on the outcome of the elections to the National Assembly for Wales. In all three elections, no party secured a majority of seats and therefore the final outcome was either a minority administration (1999 and 2001) or a coalition (2007). Given that Labour polled over 50 per cent of Welsh votes in the 1997 general election, it might not have been unreasonable to have predicted a clear victory for Labour in the first devolved election in Wales in 1999.

Unlike in Scotland, there are no other proportional electoral systems used in Wales that may be deployed for the purposes of comparison with the additional member system. A number of observations can be made, however. In the first instance, the ratio of constituency members to additional, regional members (a ratio of 2:1) means a less than proportional result. The Liberal Democrats have been under-represented in all three Assembly elections in Wales. In 2007, they polled 14.7 per cent of **first votes** and yet received only 10 per cent of the seats. In terms of the number of seats involved, winning six rather than nine seats may not seem significant, but in percentage terms it would have represented a 50 per cent increase in seats for the Liberal Democrats in the National Assembly for Wales.

Earlier in the chapter mention was also made of the fortunes of small parties who have not been able to make the breakthrough in terms of seats that a system such as the additional member system is supposed to facilitate. In 2007, the British National Party, the United Kingdom Independence Party and the Greens were able to achieve 11.4 per cent of the **second votes** between them. Given the relatively small number of additional members (twenty), none of these parties was able to muster sufficient votes in its own right to gain a seat.

✔ What you should have learnt from reading this chapter

- An understanding of the background and recent history of voting behaviour in Wales

- A knowledge of the background to devolution in Wales

- The results of the three elections to the National Assembly for Wales

- Evaluation of elections to the National Assembly for Wales and to Westminster

- The fortunes of the political parties in elections to the National Assembly for Wales

- The use of the additional member system

🔍 Glossary of key terms

Administrative devolution The situation where the devolved assembly has the power to run key public services, such as education and health. This is a rather limited form of devolution and many nationalist politicians complain that it amounts to little more power than is given to local councils. Indeed, during the 1997 referendums on devolution, Tony Blair, in an unguarded remark, described the devolved bodies as 'glorified parish councils', clearly a description that must have jarred with nationalists in Scotland and in Wales.

Coalition A partnership of two or more political parties in government. This normally occurs when a single political party falls short of a parliamentary majority to form a government on its own. This is not the norm in British politics. In countries operating proportional voting systems, however, they are quite common.

Financial devolution Where the devolved body has the power to levy taxation and to vary the rate of income tax. Controversially, this power was granted to the Scottish Parliament, by dint of a separate question in the referendum. Much to the annoyance of Welsh nationalists, this power was not included in the proposals for devolution in Wales.

First vote In the additional member system, voters cast two votes. The first vote is the one cast in a constituency using the simple plurality method of voting.

Hypothetical election This is not a real election. Public opinion bodies often ask the question, 'If there were a general election held tomorrow, which party would you support?' The studies cited in this chapter asked voters who had participated in elections to the National Assembly for Wales to declare how they would have voted if there had been a general election held at the same time. Those who had participated in a general election were also asked to declare how they would have voted if there had been an election to the National Assembly for Wales held at the same time.

Legislative devolution is where the devolved body has the power to make primary legislation. This was afforded to the Scottish Parliament but not to the National Assembly for Wales. Nationalists in Wales have been calling for greater powers of devolution to be handed to the devolved administration in Cardiff.

Minority government When a party seeks to govern without a majority of seats and does not enter into a coalition with another party. In such circumstances, the government is vulnerable to defeat in votes in the House of Commons. Between February and October 1974, and between 1976 and 1979, Britain had a minority Labour government.

North–south divide A feature of electoral behaviour which first came to prominence in the 1970s and 1980s in UK elections. Labour tended to do better in northern England and Scotland, with the Conservatives doing better the further south in England the constituency was located. In Wales, something of a north-south divide has also been apparent, this time affecting the Labour Party and Plaid Cymru, the Welsh nationalists. Labour has tended to be better supported in the valleys of industrial and urban south Wales, whilst Plaid Cymru has prospered more in the north of Wales, which is mainly Welsh-speaking.

Plaid Cymru The name of the nationalist party in Wales.

Second-order elections A term used to describe elections where voters might choose to use a protest vote against the government in Westminster. Local council elections or elections to the European Parliament are often described as such. If voters are seen to vote in a devolved election on the basis of devolved rather than UK-wide issues and differently to the way they would in a general election, then the elections concerned would not be described as second-order elections.
Second vote In the additional member system, voters cast two votes. The second vote is based on the party list proportional system with the voter casting a vote for the party and not an individual candidate.

? Likely examination questions

Distinguish between the outcomes of the three elections to the National Assembly for Wales.

'Nationalism has made less of an impact on Welsh politics than it has on Scottish politics.' Discuss.

Helpful websites

National Assembly for Wales

http://www.assemblywales.org/index.htm

Welsh Electoral Commission

http://www.electoralcommission.org.uk/wales

Suggestions for further reading

V. Bogdanor, *Devolution in the United Kingdom*, Oxford University Press, 1999.

R. Deacon and A. Sandry, *Devolution in the United Kingdom*, Edinburgh University Press, 2007.

P. Norris, *Electoral Change since 1945*, Blackwell, 1997.

A. Trench (ed.), *Devolution and Power in the United Kingdom*, Manchester University Press, 2007.

R. Wyn Jones and R. Scully, 'Devolution and Electoral Politics in Scotland and Wales', *Publius: The Journal of Federalism*, vol. 36, no. 1, pp. 115–34, Oxford University Press.

Voting in Northern Ireland

Contents

Overview

The Blair government held a referendum on devolution in Ulster in May 1998, the result of which means that Northern Ireland has elected its own Assembly since June 1998. As part of the new constitutional settlement in Northern Ireland, the new Assembly has been elected using a different electoral system to the one that the voters of Ulster use to elect MPs to the House of Commons.

This chapter explores the differences between in voting in general elections in Northern Ireland and in those for the devolved Assembly. In addition, there will be an examination of the fortunes of the main political parties in Northern Ireland. Finally, there will be an assessment of how the single transferable vote system has affected the outcome of the devolved elections in Northern Ireland.

Key issues to be covered in this chapter

- The background to the unique political situation in Northern Ireland
- The basis of voting behaviour in Northern Ireland elections
- An examination of the similarities and differences in Northern Ireland Assembly and Westminster elections
- How the main political parties in Northern Ireland have fared in devolved elections
- An assessment of the single transferable vote in Northern Ireland

Background

Studies of voting behaviour in the United Kingdom normally attempt to deal with Northern Ireland separately, with a number choosing to ignore it altogether. Any cursory observation of the political situation in Northern Ireland should answer the question why. While **psephological** studies of Britain charted the influence of class and partisan alignment on support for the Conservative parties, other forces had shaped the faces of the political parties in Northern Ireland. Indeed, all of the analysis in Chapter 5 of this book was confined to voting behaviour in Britain (that is, the United Kingdom excluding Northern Ireland).

While social class was the main determinant of party support for most people living in England, Scotland and Wales, religion was the key factor in Northern Ireland. The main political parties there are not Labour, Conservative and Liberal Democrat; instead they are labelled **unionist** and **nationalist**. These labels describe the stances that the parties hold on the issue of Northern Ireland being part of the United Kingdom. Unionists believe that Northern Ireland should remain part of the union; nationalists look towards Eire (the Republic of Ireland) in the south, believing in a united Ireland.

This situation is one of the long-term effects of the **partition** of Ireland in 1921. Twenty-six of the thirty-two original counties of Ireland would eventually form Eire. The remaining six counties in the north-east were largely Protestant and they remained part of the UK as Northern Ireland. However, out of the population of one and a half million, about one-third was Roman Catholic, many of whom wanted to be part of the Irish Republic. This, in essence, was the crucible in which the **Troubles** of the 1970s and 1980s would burn.

The government of Northern Ireland, based in Belfast, was always a unionist one and many Catholic nationalists believed that they had no political say and that they were discriminated against by those in political power. The biggest political party on the unionist side was for many decades the Ulster Unionist Party, and for much of its history it was allied to the UK Conservative Party (indeed, the official title of the latter was, up until the 1970s, the Conservative and Unionist Party). The UUP could be counted on to support the Conservatives in the House of Commons and its MPs would sit on the same side of the House as Conservative MPs. The biggest political party on the nationalist side was the Social Democratic and Labour Party, which allied itself most of the time to the British Labour Party. Its MPs would sit on the same side of the House of Commons as Labour MPs.

Although Labour and the Conservatives did not field candidates in Northern Ireland, they were allied to political parties that did. In the eyes of most unionists, therefore, the Conservatives could be trusted to guard against threats to Northern Ireland's place in the union. Nationalists saw Labour not so much as the deliverer of a united Ireland, but as a party that was committed to ending the inequality and injustices that they believed were ingrained in the politics of the province.

In the event it was the Conservative government of Edward Heath that abolished the Northern Ireland government in **Stormont** and introduced **direct rule** to the province at the height of the Troubles in 1972. Many see this as a recognition that the devolved government of Northern Ireland was incapable of dealing with the crisis in an even-handed manner and that it had lost the consent of a growing number in the nationalist community. All attempts to resolve the Northern Ireland political problem have attempted to deal with one stark fact, mentioned at the beginning of the chapter: the majority of the population of Northern Ireland are Protestant and in Northern Ireland the majority of voters have voted according to their religion. Any political settlement in Northern Ireland had to overcome the prospect of a permanent unionist government.

By the 1970s, both Conservative and Labour governments in Westminster were trying to find political solutions to the governance of Northern Ireland. These attempts may be classified in two ways. The first represents those initiatives which sought to reintroduce some form of devolution for Northern Ireland. The second is the attempts to reform aspects of the local government election process. The latter included the introduction of proportional representation for elections to local councils in Northern Ireland (also later introduced for Northern Ireland elections to the European Parliament).

The system chosen for these elections was the single transferable vote. The choice of this system was quite deliberate. In Chapter 4 it was mentioned that one of the consequences of STV is that it usually leads to the election of representatives from more than one political tradition in the same multi-member constituency. In a divided and distrustful society, this sort of cross-party representation is an essential prerequisite for the popular consent of the political system.

Successive UK governments have worked with the UUP and the SDLP in order to find a political solution to the Troubles in Northern Ireland and these parties were, in the eyes of many of the more hard-line nationalists and unionists, betraying the causes for which they should have been fighting. From the 1970s, more unionists turned to the Democratic Unionist Party, founded by Ian Paisley in 1971, promising 'no surrender' of the cause of unionism. Increasingly, large numbers of nationalists abandoned the SDLP in favour of Sinn Féin, which claimed to fight for a united Ireland. By the 1990s, public opinion appeared to be polarising away from the centre and towards the extremes of Northern Ireland politics.

However, there was a political breakthrough in 1992, when the UK Prime Minister, John Major, and his Irish counterpart, Albert Reynolds, signed the so-called '**Downing Street Declaration**', which would pave the way two years later to a prolonged IRA cease-fire and eventually to the signing of the **Good Friday Agreement** in 1998 which contained proposals for the return of self-government in the form of the Northern Ireland Assembly.

Interestingly, the provisions of the Good Friday Agreement bear close resemblance to the **Sunningdale Agreement**, negotiated by the Heath government early in the Troubles and signed in December 1973. Twenty-four years on and thousands of deaths later, Seamus Mallon, deputy leader of the SDLP, suggested that the Good Friday Agreement was 'Sunningdale for slow learners'. In 1974, however, the only parties signed up were the UUP and the SDLP. Both the Democratic Unionist Party (DUP) and Sinn Féin refused to support it. Indeed, it was effectively sunk by a workers' protest in the same year, stirred up by Ian Paisley and his DUP. The Good Friday Agreement, in contrast, was supported by Sinn Féin; the DUP was still hostile to the deal although it did not boycott the subsequent elections.

Voting in Northern Ireland Assembly elections

There have been three elections to the Northern Ireland Assembly: in 1998, 2003 and 2007. The political settlement that was part of the

Good Friday Agreement established that a future devolved government in Northern Ireland had to involve **power sharing**, in other words, it must contain members of both the unionist and the nationalist traditions. This effectively meant that the leading unionist party and the leading nationalist party would form the **Northern Ireland Executive** (in other words, the government of Northern Ireland). It was clear early on that the two parties most committed to the accord were the UUP and the SDLP. The Official Unionists in particular had invested a lot in the agreement and were accused by the DUP of making too many concessions and of sitting down with terrorists.

The common assumption was that it would be the UUP and the SDLP that would form the first power-sharing executive. As mentioned earlier in the chapter, political behaviour was changing in Northern Ireland and although most voters supported parties within their own religious tradition, recent electoral trends had shown that support for the more moderate parties within each was being challenged. Both the DUP and Sinn Féin were making gains in various electoral contests. Figure 8.1 shows the changing support for the four main political parties in Northern Ireland between the 1970 and 2005 general elections.

The graph clearly shows a decline in the fortunes of the SDLP and a rise in those of Sinn Féin from the late 1990s (Sinn Féin contested its first Westminster elections in 1983; its elected MPs have refused to sit in the House of Commons since they would have to swear an oath of allegiance to the UK monarch). A similar pattern may be discerned for the UUP and the DUP. By 2005, the DUP was the leading unionist party in Northern Ireland and Sinn Féin had become the leading force of nationalism in the province.

The advent of devolved government showed that there was certainly no guarantee that the expectations of who would form the first devolved government in Northern Ireland in more than a quarter of a century would be realised. If the DUP had won the most unionist seats in the Assembly, there was a distinct chance that it would refuse to be involved in any power-sharing arrangement with nationalists. If this happened then the chances were that the whole of the Good Friday Agreement would have unravelled.

In the event it was the Official Unionists that came top of the party votes in the first elections to the Northern Ireland Assembly in

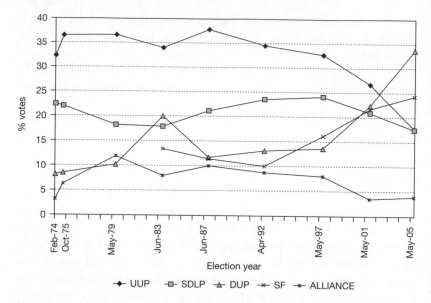

Chart created from data compiled from: CAIN Web Service (Conflict Archive on the INternet) http://cain.ulst.ac.uk/index.html

Figure 8.1 General election results in Northern Ireland 1974–2005

June 1998. The SDLP came second and the first Northern Ireland Executive came into existence shortly afterwards with David Trimble of the UUP as First Minister and Seamus Mallon of the SDLP as Deputy First Minister. Table 8.1 shows the full results of the 1998 elections to the Northern Ireland Assembly. The parties that went on to form the Northern Ireland Executive are in bold.

Unlike the Scottish Parliament and the National Assembly for Wales, the history of devolution in Northern Ireland since this time has been quite a troubled and turbulent one. The first elections did see the return of devolved government to the province, but the Assembly was suspended on no fewer than four occasions between 2000 and 2007. The longest of these suspensions lasted nearly five years (October 2002 to May 2007) and the results of the Northern Ireland Assembly elections in 2003 resulted in the DUP topping the poll and refusing to accept the nomination for government by Sinn Féin, which beat the SDLP into second place. Table 8.2 shows the full results of the 2003 elections to the Northern Ireland Assembly.

Table 8.1 The 1998 elections to the Northern Ireland Assembly

Party	No. of first-preference votes	% votes	No. of seats
Social Democratic and Labour Party (SDLP)	177,963	21.96	24
Ulster Unionist Party (UUP)	172,225	21.25	28
Democratic Unionist Party (DUP)	145,917	18.01	20
Sinn Féin (SF)	142,858	17.63	18
Alliance Party of Northern Ireland (APNI)	52,636	6.50	6
United Kingdom Unionists (UKU)	36,541	4.51	5
Progressive Unionist Party (PUP)	20,634	2.55	2
NI Women's Coalition (WC)	13,019	1.61	2
Ulster Democratic Party (UDP)	8,651	1.07	0
Labour (Lab)	2,729	0.34	0
Others	37,144	4.58	3
Total	**810,317**	**100.00**	**108**

Source: CAIN Web Service (Conflict Archive on the INternet) http://cain.ulst.ac.uk/index.html

The people of Northern Ireland appeared to be losing faith in the devolution process; by increasing support for the more extreme parties in the two religious and political traditions in the province there was a fear in the UK government that citizens in Northern Ireland were turning their backs on the peace process and returning to their tribal enmities. The voices of moderation appeared to be going unheard.

The year 2003 did not result in the formation of an executive and the Northern Ireland Assembly remained suspended. The legislation governing devolution in Northern Ireland stipulates that if a First Minister cannot be chosen, then the Assembly has to be dissolved. As a consequence, the 2003 election may be seen more as

Table 8.2 The 2003 elections to the Northern Ireland Assembly

Party	No. of first-preference votes	% votes	Change % votes	No. of seats	Change no. seats
Democratic Unionist Party (DUP)	177,944	25.71	+7.70	30	+10
Sinn Féin (SF)	162,758	23.52	+5.89	24	+6
Ulster Unionist Party (UUP)	156,931	22.68	+1.43	27	+1
Social Democratic and Labour Party (SDLP)	117,547	16.99	-4.97	18	-5
Alliance Party of Northern Ireland (APNI)	25,370	3.67	-2.83	6	0
Independent (Ind)	19,256	2.78	-	1	0
Progressive Unionist Party (PUP)	8,032	1.16	-1.39	1	-1
Northern Ireland Women's Coalition (NIWC)	5,785	0.84	-0.77	0	-2
United Kingdom Unionists (UKUP)	5,700	0.82	-3.69	1	0
Independent Unionist (Ind U)	5,387	0.78	-	0	-5
United Unionist Coalition (UUC)	2,705	0.39	-	0	0
Green Party (Green)	2,688	0.39	+0.30	0	0
Socialist Environmental Alliance (SEA)	2,394	0.35	-	0	0

Party	Votes	%	Change	Seats
Conservative Party (Con)	1,604	0.23	+0.03	0
Workers' Party (WP)	1,407	0.20	-0.04	0
Northern Ireland Unionist Party (NIUP)	1,350	0.20	-	-4
Independent Nationalist (Ind N)	1,121	0.16	-	0
Socialist Party (SP)	343	0.05	-	0
Independent Labour (Ind L)	162	0.02	+0.01	0
Vote For Yourself Party (VFYP)	124	0.02	-	0
Ulster Third Way (UTW)	16	0.00	-	0
Total	**692,026**	**100.00**		**108**

Source: CAIN Web Service (Conflict Archive on the INternet) http://cain.ulst.ac.uk/index.html

a virility contest for the various participants rather than something that was likely to see a return to devolved government. Throughout this period, all the powers that had been devolved to the Northern Ireland Assembly were returned to the Northern Ireland Office in London. The era of 'direct rule' had returned and hopes for devolution in Northern Ireland looked bleak.

As in the previous two chapters, a number of key questions need to be asked when analysing the outcomes of these elections. First, how do voting patterns compare between elections to the Northern Ireland Assembly and elections of Northern Ireland constituency MPs to Westminster? Secondly, are elections to the Northern Ireland Assembly **second-order elections**, in other words are they treated less seriously than elections to the House of Commons? Which political parties have done well and less well out of the use of this electoral system? Does the single transferable vote system itself affect the way in which the voters of Northern Ireland behave in elections to the Northern Ireland Assembly?

Comparing Westminster and Stormont elections

The results of the first elections to the Northern Ireland Assembly in 1998 provide an interesting picture of the relative support for the main political parties compared with how they fared in the 1997 general election. Table 8.3 illustrates this.

Perhaps the first thing to say about these figures is that they cannot be directly compared to similar tables in the previous two chapters. There is no governing party upon which to pass judgement, so there can be no analysis of a decline in Labour Party support in this first devolved election in Northern Ireland as happened when studying the first devolved elections to the Scottish Parliament and the National Assembly for Wales. There is, however, a trend in these figures. Both the front runners in the 1997 and previous general elections, the UUP and the SDLP , saw their votes fall in the first elections to the Northern Ireland Assembly. In the case of the UUP, the fall was over 10 per cent, which in just a year is a major shift in votes. The decline in the SDLP vote was less dramatic. Both the DUP and Sinn Féin saw a rise in their fortunes. Again it was the unionists rather than the nationalists that saw the more significant increase. The 1998

Table 8.3 Comparison of 1997 general election and 1998 Northern Ireland Assembly election results

	1997 general election		1998 NIA election	
	% votes	Seats	% votes	Seats
UUP	32.7	10	21.2	28
SDLP	24.1	3	22.0	24
DUP	13.6	2	18.0	20
Sinn Fein	16.1	2	17.6	18
Others	13.5	1	21.2	18

Table created from data compiled from: CAIN Web Service (Conflict Archive on the INternet) http://cain.ulst.ac.uk/index.html

Northern Ireland Assembly elections were perhaps a portent of things to come with the stirrings of hardline unionism happening so soon after the success of the Good Friday Agreement.

Perhaps the big story of the first devolved elections to the new Northern Ireland Assembly was the performance of the smaller parties. It would appear that a combination of an election based around devolved issues and a proportional electoral system led to a significant increase in the vote for smaller parties. One of these parties, the Alliance Party, had been fighting Westminster elections since the 1970s without winning a single seat, despite on occasions polling more than 10 per cent of the vote. Although the popularity of the Alliance Party (which had sought to attract voters from across the religious divide in Northern Ireland) had been in decline, it was still able to gain six seats in the new Assembly.

In all, eighteen out of the one hundred and eight Assembly seats were won by these smaller parties compared to only one out of the eighteen Northern Ireland seats in the House of Commons in 1997. This compares very favourably to either of the results of the first elections to the Scottish Parliament and the National Assembly for Wales, where virtually all the seats were won by the political parties that had already established representation in the House of Commons. To a great extent, the Scottish and Welsh results seemed to amount

Table 8.4 Comparison of 2001 general election and 2003 Northern Ireland Assembly election results

	2001 general election		2003 NIA election	
Party	% votes	Seats	% votes	Seats
UUP	26.7	6	22.7	27
SDLP	20.9	3	17.0	18
DUP	22.4	5	25.7	30
Sinn Féin	21.7	4	23.5	24
Others	8.3	0	11.1	9

Table created from data compiled from: CAIN Web Service (Conflict Archive on the INternet) http://cain.ulst.ac.uk/index.html

more to a redistribution of seats between these parties than to fair representation for all parties. The Northern Ireland results, however, appear to have meant that more small political parties were represented in the Northern Ireland Assembly. The extent to which the different voting system used in Northern Ireland contributed to this outcome will be discussed later in the chapter.

The second Assembly elections took place in 2003. Table 8.4 offers the results of these elections and the results of the 2001 general election in Northern Ireland.

The trends first noted in the analysis of the results of the 1998 Northern Ireland Assembly elections appear to continue in 2003. Both the UUP and the SDLP saw their share of the vote decline across both sets of elections. Significantly, however, the Assembly result put the DUP ahead in a Northern Ireland election for the first time. The DUP also accounts for another of the trends in these results, concerning the performance of the smaller parties. Most of the DUP's seat gains in the Assembly were not from the UUP (it lost just one Assembly seat in 2003). Instead these gains seem to have come at the expense of minor unionist party representation. Overall the smaller parties saw a combined decline of 10 per cent in the Northern Ireland vote in 2003 and the number of seats was halved from eighteen to just nine.

Of course, this analysis is to some degree pointless in that it did not lead to the gathering of a new Northern Ireland Assembly or the formation of an executive. However, from a psephological perspective, these results confirm that public opinion in Northern Ireland was indeed polarising and the main beneficiaries of this were parties that no one could reasonably imagine would ever want to share power with each other. The backdrop to all this was a suspended Assembly and, despite Tony Blair's statement that there was 'no plan B' for devolution in Northern Ireland, one of the major successes of his time in office looked to be on the brink of collapse.

One of the questions asked in the previous two chapters was regarding the extent to which voters in Scotland and Wales treated the elections to their devolved Parliament and Assembly as second-order elections. The measure that was used in both Chapter 6 and Chapter 7 was to analyse the data from surveys that compared voting in real and hypothetical elections. One of the reasons for such analysis is to ascertain whether voting in devolved elections is to some degree a protest vote against the governing party in Westminster and that these elections constitute second-order elections. In the case of the Scottish Parliament and the National Assembly for Wales there is some evidence to suggest that voters voted differently in different types of election and that this was not simply expressing a protest vote, rather voters were voting on issues that they thought were relevant to the elections that were being contested.

There is a major difficulty in performing the same analysis in the case of Northern Ireland. The major UK-wide political parties do not take part in Northern Ireland elections. The Conservatives, in an ill-fated enterprise, have fielded candidates in Northern Ireland constituencies since 1992 and their biggest share of the vote was in 1992 when they polled 44,600 out of a total of 785,000 votes cast in the province. The last occasion when the party took part in Northern Ireland constituency elections was in 2005, when it polled just 2,718 out of a total of nearly 724,000 votes. There is really very little that the Assembly elections can tell us about how they compare with general elections.

Perhaps the salience of these different types of elections may be gauged according to their respective levels of participation. Generally a high electoral turnout signifies that voters are interested in the issues involved in the election as well its outcome. General elections

Table 8.5 Comparison of electoral turnout

General Election	% turnout	Assembly election	% turnout
1997	67.3	1998	69.9
2001	68.7	2003	63.0
2005	63.5	2007	62.9

Table created from data compiled from: CAIN Web Service (Conflict Archive on the INternet) http://cain.ulst.ac.uk/index.html

tend to have higher turnouts than local government elections, for example. This is another of the reasons why the latter are sometimes regarded as second-order elections. Often electors cast their vote in order to register a protest against the government in Westminster. As was mentioned earlier, it is difficult to gauge the qualitative nature of votes in Northern Ireland; it is, however, possible to examine the difference between the percentages of votes cast. Table 8.5 shows the percentage turnouts in the general elections of 1997, 2001 and 2005 compared with the elections to the Northern Ireland Assembly in 1998, 2003 and 2007.

In two out of three of the Assembly elections, the turnout is lower, but in the first election, in 1998, it is higher. The differences are not remarkable, however, and do not match the lower turnouts in elections to the Scottish Parliament and the National Assembly for Wales. This might perhaps suggest that these elections are not treated any less seriously than general elections in the minds of Northern Ireland's voters. An alternative analysis might be that voters in the province take these elections just as seriously because of what is at stake. Northern Ireland endured nearly forty years of violence, with a whole generation growing up in the shadow of terrorists and a permanent military presence. In this sense many in Northern Ireland might have thought the stakes in all of the above elections to be rather high.

Much of the analysis so far has been confined to the first two elections to the Northern Ireland Assembly. The following section looks at the outcome of the third election, in 2007.

Box 8.1 The 2007 election to the Northern Ireland Assembly

Table 8.6 provides data showing the relative performance of the political parties in the general election in 2005 and the 2007 election to the Northern Ireland Assembly.

The outcome of both these elections would seem to confirm the process of realignment that appears to be taking place in Northern Ireland. Although the DUP did not quite match the share of the vote in the 2007 Assembly election that they managed in the general election in 2005, this was still an impressive result, representing an increase of just under 5 per cent on their showing in the Assembly elections in 2003. The big picture is the continued decline of the UUP and SDLP. The decline in the UUP share of the Assembly vote was just under 3 per cent; however, compared to the 2003 Assembly elections, its share of the vote fell by more than 7 per cent. Figure 8.2 shows the changes in support for the UUP and the DUP between 1997 and 2007.

In spite of the increase in support that the UUP enjoyed in the general election of 2001, the overall trend is one of decline. The dip in support for the DUP in 2007 was not matched with a corresponding rise in the UUP vote, which probably means that the likely beneficiaries were some of the smaller unionist parties taking advantage of the single transferable vote. Smaller parties increased their share of the vote by 2.5 per cent between the Assembly elections of 2003 and 2007.

The SDLP saw a much steadier decline between the general election of 2005 and the Assembly election of 2007. Again, the longer-term picture says more. Between the general elections of 1997 and 2005, the SDLP's share of the vote declined from 24.1 per cent to 17.5 per cent. The figures over the three elections to the Assembly tell a similar story (a decline from 22 per cent in 1998 to 15.2 per cent in 2007).

Sinn Féin's support has seen an increase in each successive election it has fought since 1997. Figure 8.3 illustrates the reversal of fortunes of Sinn Féin and the SDLP during this period.

A deal was struck in November 2006 to break the deadlock in Northern Ireland's political system. The St Andrews Agreement paved the way for a return to power sharing, and following the elections of 2007, a power-sharing executive was formed between the DUP and Sinn Féin with Ian Paisley becoming First Minister and Martin McGuinness Deputy First Minister. This alliance would have been unheard of even two years earlier. The second phase of power sharing in Northern Ireland since the Good Friday Agreement has now lasted more than two years.

Table 8.6 Comparison of 2005 general election and 2007 Northern Ireland Assembly election results

	2005 general election		2007 NIA election	
	% votes	Seats	% votes	Seats
UUP	17.7	1	14.9	18
SDLP	17.5	3	15.2	16
DUP	33.7	9	30.1	36
Sinn Féin	24.3	5	26.2	28
Others	6.8	0	13.6	10

Table created from data compiled from: CAIN Web Service (Conflict Archive on the INternet) http://cain.ulst.ac.uk/index.html

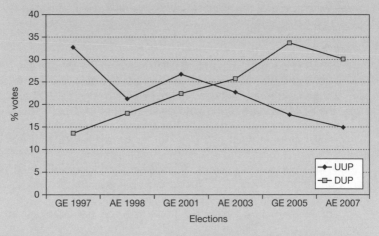

Chart created from data compiled from: CAIN Web Service (Conflict Archive on the INternet) http://cain.ulst.ac.uk/index.html

Figure 8.2 Electoral support for the UUP and the DUP 1997–2007

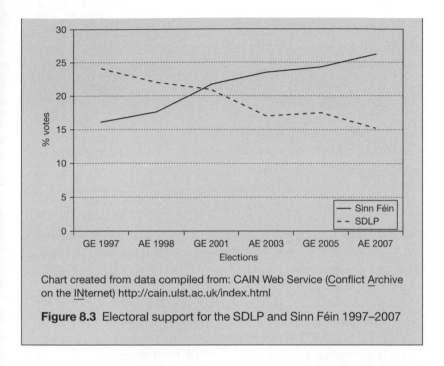

Chart created from data compiled from: CAIN Web Service (Conflict Archive on the INternet) http://cain.ulst.ac.uk/index.html

Figure 8.3 Electoral support for the SDLP and Sinn Féin 1997–2007

The performance of political parties

As in the case of the Scottish Parliament and the National Assembly for Wales, a four- party system is clearly at work in Northern Ireland. Unlike Scotland and Wales, all these parties are peculiar to Northern Ireland's political setting and the province remains relatively unaffected by the party dynamics in the rest of the United Kingdom. It is clear that the political dynamics in Ulster are altering and that there is a clear change in the fortunes of all the political parties in the province.

The Democratic Unionist Party

This party was established in 1971 to stand up for the rights of the Protestant community in Northern Ireland. Its co-founder, Ian Paisley, believed that the UUP could not be trusted because it was likely to agree to a settlement of Northern Ireland's problems which would undermine the position of unionists in the province. The

DUP remained a relatively small political party in Northern Ireland for the first part of its life and it appeared, at the time of the signing of the Good Friday Agreement in 1998, that it was the party out of step with public opinion in the province (the other three main parties were all signatories). Yet the first elections to the Northern Ireland Assembly in 1998 saw a rise in the vote for the DUP and a major fall in support for the UUP (based on their shares of the vote in the 1997 general election).

The results of the May 1998 referendum on the Good Friday Agreement were interesting because although there was a 'Yes' vote of over 70 per cent in favour, there was a much higher level of support among nationalists than among unionists. Perhaps the DUP had managed to tap into a seam of distrust in unionist thinking, a suspicion that too many concessions were being made to the nation-alists and concern that respectable politicians were sitting around the negotiating table with former terrorists.

In the course of a decade, the DUP was able to replace the UUP as the main unionist force in Northern Ireland. This placed the party in a position to deal a devastating blow to power sharing and the entire peace process. If the utterances of Ian Paisley in the past were anything to go by, then the Good Friday Agreement was dead and buried.

The reason for Ian Paisley's decision to form a power-sharing executive with Sinn Féin can only be a matter for speculation here. Perhaps he wanted his and his party's legacy to be one of peace. Whatever the reason, to have the more hardline of the unionist parties in government might settle the worries many Protestants in Northern Ireland have about doing deals with nationalists. Perhaps this situation is best summed up by the saying from across the Atlantic that 'only Nixon could go to China'.

Sinn Féin

If the DUP was a reluctant part of the Northern Ireland peace process, the involvement of Sinn Féin is perhaps more surprising. As the political wing of the **IRA**, the party was committed to a united Ireland, and many of its members had played an active part in the paramilitary campaign against the presence of the British army patrolling the streets of Belfast and other towns in Northern

Ireland. It had started contesting Westminster elections in 1983 but, as mentioned earlier, refused to take up the seats it won in the House of Commons. Sinn Féin's electoral support declined during the 1980s and early 1990s. It is from about this time that the party began behind-the-scenes negotiations which would eventually lead to an IRA ceasefire in August 1994. The tactic of embracing the democratic route has proved to be a successful one. Sinn Féin's share of the Northern Ireland vote in the 1992 general election was just over 10 per cent. By 2005 the party had polled nearly 25 per cent of the vote.

The prize for Sinn Féin is that it is now the main nationalist force in Northern Ireland, playing a major role in the governance of the province. Conversely, it appears that the party has settled for something far short of the united Ireland for which it had for so long campaigned. By accepting the terms of the Good Friday Agreement, the party, officially at least, has accepted the constitutional position of Northern Ireland and the right of the citizens of the province to decide whether it remains within the United Kingdom or becomes part of a united Ireland in the future. Perhaps it is this latter prospect that Sinn Féin hopes to see realised.

The Ulster Unionist Party

For this party, once the major force in Northern Ireland, devolution has been accompanied by a quite rapid decline in fortunes. The extent to which the UUP has declined might best be served by delving back into history. In 1969, the last elections to the old Stormont Parliament (axed by Ted Heath in 1972) took place. In that contest, the UUP polled over 48 per cent of the vote (more than 35 per cent more than its nearest rival) and won thirty-six of the fifty-two seats in the Assembly. By 2007 only around 15 per cent of Northern Ireland voters supported the UUP. There is something of a cruel paradox in this; the UUP was one of the parties that was most committed to the creation of a power-sharing administration in the run-up to the Good Friday Agreement in 1998. The political price that the UUP has paid for helping to find a political solution to the Troubles in Northern Ireland has been a high one.

This declining vote has occurred both in elections to the Northern Ireland Assembly and in general elections. Analysis of the figures shows that until 2001, the party was doing better in elections to the House of Commons than to the Northern Ireland Assembly. Indeed, in the general election of that year, the UUP saw an increase in its share of the vote achieved in the 1998 Assembly election. Support for the party after 2001, however, has continued to decline.

It is too early to say whether this decline is terminal and the UUP will become one of the many minor unionist parties that exist in Northern Ireland. If there is a process of normalisation in the province, where security, terrorist and sectarian issues begin to recede, it is possible that the edge that the DUP has developed for itself on these issues over other unionist parties will be blunted. Perhaps the electoral pendulum will swing back in the direction of the UUP if the DUP fails to satisfy Northern Irish voters on more 'mundane' issues such as the economy, health and schools.

The Social Democratic and Labour Party
The SDLP was never as much of a force in Northern Irish politics as the UUP. For a period between the 1970s and the late 1990s, however, it was the most important nationalist party in Northern Ireland. The party averaged over one-fifth of Northern Irish votes in general elections between 1974 and 2001, reaching a peak of just under a quarter in the 1997 general election. As the line graph above, charting the changing fortunes of the SDLP and Sinn Féin, shows, 1997 was something of a high water mark. By the Assembly elections of 2007, support for the SDLP had fallen to its lowest point for over thirty years.

It would appear that the SDLP were prone to the same forces on the nationalist side of the Northern Ireland divide that had affected the UUP on the unionist side. In other words, more hardline nationalist ideas were resonating more strongly with opinion within the Catholic nationalist community. The SDLP had never been seriously threatened by other nationalist parties until ten years ago. There has long been a number of unionist parties to challenge the primacy of the UUP. Nationalists have in the main been content to support the SDLP. What has happened to nationalist public opinion to have led to the decline in SDLP support?

Along with David Trimble (leader of the UUP in the 1990s) the leader of the SDLP, John Hume, was the joint winner of the 1998

Nobel Peace Prize for their work on the Good Friday Agreement. Faced with a hardening of opinion within the unionist community behind the DUP, however, was there a mirror-like response among nationalist voters? The SDLP's steepest decline was between the general election of 2001 and the Northern Ireland Assembly election of 2003. This was also the time when the Assembly had been suspended and when the future of devolution looked bleak. In such circumstances many nationalist voters must have wondered whether the Assembly would survive. If the Northern Ireland Assembly were to fail, the main question would be regarding what would replace it. Perhaps just as important for nationalists as for unionists would have been to decide which political party was best equipped to defend their interests in a time of great political uncertainty. Unionist voters came to decide that the DUP would be that party. Nationalist voters also appeared to do the same in supporting Sinn Féin. In doing so, they rejected the long-time proponent of democratic nationalism.

The impact of the single transferable vote

There has already been some discussion in this chapter and in Chapter 4 about the impact of the single transferable vote (STV) system on the political process of Northern Ireland. The bitterness that has long existed between Protestant and Catholic, and unionist and nationalist required such a system. STV lends itself to ensuring that in a multi-member constituency, representatives from across the political divide are elected. This is important given that traditionally it is unlikely that nationalist voters would seek redress from their representative if he or she were a unionist. As mentioned earlier in this chapter, STV has already served Northern Ireland well in local elections as well as in the province's elections to the European Parliament (Northern Ireland was the first part of the United Kingdom to operate a proportional voting system for some of its elections).

Another factor may also be reinforced at this point. In the previous two chapters, there has been some discussion about the position of the smaller political parties in Scotland and Wales. In both these countries it would appear that the additional member system has not worked sufficiently well to provide smaller parties with better representation. This was not such a big factor in Scotland, where parties other than the 'big four' only polled 22 per cent of the vote, achieving 2 out of the 129 MSPs in the Scottish Parliament (as opposed to the notional and proportional 2.89). Wales was a different matter, however, where 8.3 per cent of Welsh voters supported smaller parties in the 2007 Assembly election, securing only one of the sixty Assembly seats. A proportional result would have given these parties six seats in the Assembly. The position of smaller parties appeared to be better in Northern Ireland, where smaller parties secured ten of the one hundred and eight Assembly seats on 13.6 per cent of the vote. Although these parties should have secured another four seats proportionally, the disparity is far less than that in Wales.

One possible reason for this is the way in which the single transferable vote enables voters to rank the candidates on the ballot paper in order of preference and for transfers of surplus or eliminated votes to be made from candidate to candidate. This goes to show that some proportional systems are more proportional than others.

. . . .

✔ What you should have learnt from reading this chapter

- An understanding of the recent political developments in Northern Ireland

- An understanding of the basis of voting behaviour in Northern Ireland elections

- The main similarities and differences between Westminster and Northern Ireland Assembly elections

- A knowledge of the background to devolution in Northern Ireland

- The results of the three elections to the Northern Ireland Assembly

- The fortunes of the political parties in elections to the Northern Ireland Assembly

- The use of the single transferable voting system

🔎 Glossary of key terms

Direct rule A term that refers to the situation when devolved government is either suspended or ended and powers for the running of a particular area are returned to Westminster and a government department. The government of Northern Ireland, which was established in 1921, ran the affairs of the province until 1972 when it was abolished by the UK government. Its powers were taken over by the Northern Ireland Office.

Downing Street Declaration The agreement between the governments in London and Dublin. It set out a set of principles about Northern Ireland, including that the people of Northern Ireland should decide their own political future and that neither the UK nor the Irish governments had any strategic interest in the province.

Good Friday Agreement The agreement between the UK and Irish governments along with three of the main political parties in Northern Ireland. The agreement, also known as the Belfast Agreement, included provisions to establish a Northern Ireland Assembly, a power-sharing executive and procedures for the decommissioning of terrorist weapons and to reform the way that Northern Ireland was policed.

IRA An abbreviation for the Irish Republican Army, which wanted to see the six counties of Northern Ireland joined with the twenty-six counties of the Irish Republic. The IRA's provisional wing was responsible for a number of terrorist attacks from the 1970s to the 1990s. The political wing of the organisation was Sinn Féin and a number of former paramilitary figures from the provisional IRA went on to renounce violence and strive for a political solution for Northern Ireland.

Nationalist A term to denote those people in Northern Ireland who have traditionally sought a united Ireland in preference to the province remaining part of the United Kingdom. Some hardline republican nationalists (such as the IRA) were willing to use violence to achieve their goal. Others, such as the SDLP, preferred the democratic path.

Northern Ireland Executive The name of the government of Northern Ireland as established by the Good Friday Agreement. This executive would effectively comprise departments which would be responsible for most of Northern Ireland's public services. It would be headed by a First Minister and a Deputy First Minister.

Partition In response to growing calls for Irish independence, the government of Lloyd George allowed twenty-six of the thirty-two counties to become the Irish Free State (this would later become Eire, or the Irish Republic). The remaining six, predominantly Protestant, counties remained in the United Kingdom and were given a devolved government.

Power sharing The Good Friday Agreement established that a devolved government in Northern Ireland had to involve both the unionist and the nationalist traditions. This effectively meant that the leading unionist party and the leading nationalist party would form the Northern Ireland Executive.

Psephological Relating to the study of voting behaviour and elections.

Second-order elections A term used to describe elections where voters might choose to use a protest vote against the government in Westminster. Local council elections or elections to the European

Parliament are often described as such. If voters are seen to vote in a devolved election on the basis of devolved rather than UK-wide issues and differently to the way they would in a general election, then the elections concerned would not be described as second-order elections.

Stormont The building just outside Belfast housing the original devolved Assembly which sat between the early 1920s and the early 1970s. It was again chosen to be the seat of Northern Ireland's devolved government following the Good Friday Agreement and the referendum in 1998.

Sunningdale Agreement This was an early attempt at resolving the conflict in Northern Ireland and bringing an end to the Troubles there. The Good Friday Agreement bears a great resemblance to Sunningdale, including a Northern Ireland Assembly and a power-sharing executive.

Troubles A term used to describe the period after 1969 and up until the 1990s when paramilitary organisations were responsible for thousands of deaths of civilians, police officers and army personnel. It was also a time when there was a heavy military presence across the province.

Unionist A term to denote those individuals who want Northern Ireland to remain a part of the United Kingdom. As with the nationalist traditions, there are a number of strands to unionism. Some of these are political, such as parties like the UUP and the DUP. There have also been a number of paramilitary unionist groups such as the Ulster Defence Association and the Ulster Volunteer Force. Groups such as these were responsible for an increasing number of murders as the Troubles progressed.

? Likely examination questions

Why has political opinion become more polarised in Northern Ireland in recent years?

'Devolution in Northern Ireland is inherently more unstable than it is in Scotland or Wales.' Discuss.

Helpful websites

Northern Ireland Assembly website

http://www.niassembly.gov.uk/

Northern Ireland Electoral Commission

http://www.electoralcommission.org.uk/northern-ireland

Suggestions for further reading

V. Bogdanor, *Devolution in the United Kingdom*, Oxford University Press, 1999.

P. Carmichael, C. Knox and R. Osborne (eds), *Devolution and Constitutional Change in Northern Ireland*, Manchester University Press, 2007.

R. Deacon and A. Sandry, *Devolution in the United Kingdom*, Edinburgh University Press, 2007.

J. Tonge, *The New Northern Irish Politics?*, Palgrave, 2005.

A. Trench (ed.), *Devolution and Power in the United Kingdom*, Manchester University Press, 2007.

CHAPTER 9

Voting in Elections to the European Parliament

Contents

Overview

As part of its constitutional reform programme, the Blair government introduced a proportional electoral system for electing British Members of the European Parliament. This system has been in use since 1999.

This chapter explores the differences between voting in British general elections and in those for the European Parliament. In addition, there will be an examination of the fortunes of the main political parties in European elections. Finally, there will be an assessment of how the regional party list voting system has affected the outcome of elections to the European Parliament.

Key issues to be covered in this chapter

- The background to voting behaviour and elections to the European Parliament
- The distinction between Westminster elections and European elections
- How the main political parties have fared in elections to the European Parliament
- An assessment of the regional party list used for elections to the European Parliament

Background

The European Parliament is made up of 736 seats from the 27 EU member states. The number of representatives from each member state is determined by the size of its population. Since the **reunification** of the country in 1990, Germany has sent the biggest contingent of ninety-nine Members of the European Parliament (MEPs). Malta, with the smallest population in the European Union, has five, the fewest number of MEPs in the European Parliament. Members of the European Parliament do not sit in the chamber in national groups; rather they sit in party factions. Until recently the Conservatives sat with the group that included the German Christian Democrats. Labour MEPs sit with the socialist grouping of MEPs. The UK now has seventy-two MEPs.

There have been a total of seven elections to the European Parliament and the government of each member state determines the manner in which its MEPs are elected. Back in the 1970s, when these elections were first being planned in the UK, the Liberal Party had hoped to use its influence on the minority Labour government of James Callaghan to run the elections using a proportional voting system. The idea met stiff resistance from Labour MPs, and the first and three subsequent elections were run using the same voting system that was used to elect members of the House of Commons, the simple plurality system. As mentioned in the previous chapter, Northern Ireland's elections to the European Parliament have always been conducted using the single transferable vote electoral system.

Back in 1979, when the first direct elections were held, there were only nine EEC (now EU) states, and there were more UK Members of the European Parliament. This number has reduced in recent years as a large number of states have joined the European Union. This has been to ensure that the Parliament did not become too large and unwieldy as more states joined the EU. Throughout the 1980s and 1990s, Labour and the Conservatives held virtually all the UK seats in the European Parliament. The Liberals (later to become the Liberal Democrats) did not win a single seat in the first three elections. In the 1979 election, the Liberals polled around 1.5 million votes, rising to about 2.5 million in the 1984 election. In neither case did they win a seat in the European Parliament. Finally, in their

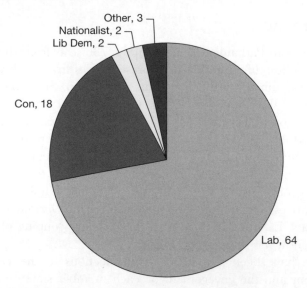

Source: D. Butler and G. Butler, *British Political Facts 1900–1994,* Macmillan, 1994.

Figure 9.1 Party share of seats in the 1994 elections to the European Parliament

fourth attempt, in 1994, and in the depths of the unpopularity of John Major's government, the Liberal Democrats won their first European Parliament seats. Figure 9.1 shows the distribution of UK seats in the European Parliament by political party.

The diagram shows the dominance of the two main political parties in these elections. The constituencies were vast (nearly eight times bigger than a typical constituency used to elect MPs to the House of Commons). Only the parties that were capable of mobilising massive numbers of votes in such large constituencies had any chance of success in these elections. Had it not been for the poor state of electoral support for the Conservatives, it is more than possible that this election too would have denied the Liberal Democrats any representation in the European Parliament. The vagaries of the simple plurality system would deal one more trick to the Liberal Democrats in the 1994 elections. The party managed to win two seats with fewer votes than in the 1984 election, when, as mentioned earlier, the party won no seats.

Great Britain was the only part of the European Union to use the simple plurality voting system to run its elections to the European Parliament. (Northern Ireland uses the single transferable vote.) To countries used to returning a plurality of political parties to represent their citizens at the European level, Great Britain must have stood out somewhat when eighty-two of its eighty-nine MEPs derived from just two political parties, which amounts to 93 per cent of the total. This massive dominance was based on a combined Labour and Conservative share of the GB vote of just 69.5 per cent in 1994. These were to be the last elections run using the simple plurality system. In 1997, the Labour government, committed to putting Britain 'at the heart of Europe', was elected, and it promised to introduce electoral reform for elections to the European Parliament. Critics of the Blair government accused it of promising electoral reform to institutions that were less important than Parliament. Blair did promise a referendum on electoral reform for elections to the House of Commons, but, as was mentioned in Chapter 4, these ideas were quietly put to one side and the country has not heard a word from the government on the issue for more than a decade

The electoral system chosen for the next election, in 1999, was the closed regional party list. The first section of Chapter 4 gives an explanation of how the system works in both theory and practice. This is the only set of elections to an existing political institution that the Blair government actually reformed. All the other proportional electoral systems are associated with new political institutions (the devolved bodies in Scotland, Wales and Northern Ireland). These elections, therefore, are the only ones where some meaningful contextual comparison can actually be made.

Voting in elections to the European Parliament since 1999

There have been three elections to the European Parliament that have been run using a proportional voting system. These were in 1999, 2004 and 2009. Unlike the elections to the Scottish Parliament, the National Assembly of Wales and the Northern Ireland Assembly, there is no executive outcome to the elections to the European Parliament. In other words, the parties are not in competition to

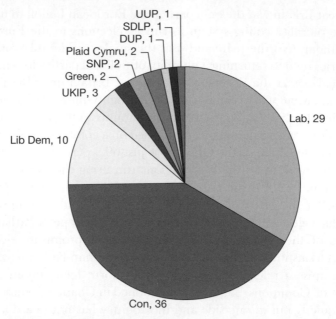

Source: http://www.ukpolitical.info/

Figure 9.2 Party share of seats in the 1999 elections to the European Parliament

form a government. Indeed, the results of the elections in the UK only form a fractional part of the overall picture across the whole of the European Union.

All three elections have been bad for the governing Labour Party, with the Conservatives winning the most seats on each occasion. The big story, as shall be seen later in the chapter, has been success for the smaller political parties. For the purposes of comparison with the above pie chart, Figure 9.2 shows the breakdown of UK party representation in the European Parliament after the 1999 elections.

Immediately one can see that the use of a proportional voting system has transformed the pattern of party distribution. The two major parties still dominate the share of the seats (in fact the Conservatives and Labour have nearly 75 per cent of the seats and just under 64 per cent of the vote), but the other political parties form a much larger percentage of the total than was the case when these elections were fought using the simple plurality voting system.

A more detailed analysis of the 2004 results can be found in the election study by David Butler and Martin Westlake.[1]

As in the previous chapter, a number of key questions need to be asked when analysing the outcomes of these elections. First, how do voting patterns compare between elections to the European Parliament and elections to the House of Commons? Secondly, are elections to the European Parliament **second-order elections**, in other words are they treated less seriously than elections to the House of Commons? Which political parties have done well and less well out of the use of this electoral system? Does the regional party list voting system itself affect the way in which the voters in the United Kingdom behave in elections to the European Parliament?

Comparing Westminster and European elections

The first elections to the European Parliament using the regional party list system were in June 1999. The pie chart above provides a clear indication of the spread of party support. How do the figures compare to a general election? Table 9.1 provides an interesting picture of the relative support for the main political parties in the elections to the European Parliament in 1999 compared with how they fared in the 1997 general election. The table excludes the election in Northern Ireland, which took place using the single transferable vote electoral system. As may be seen from the figures above, the UUP, the DUP and the SDLP each won a seat using this system.

The Conservatives found that their message with the electorate resonated in this election. The party leader at the time, William Hague, must have been very satisfied that the Conservatives appeared to be back in winning form so soon after their disastrous showing in the 1997 general election. Hague was particularly **Euro-sceptic**, and succeeding like this in an election for the European Parliament may have convinced him that this message might play well in a future general election. Indeed, in 2001, William Hague christened the Conservative Party campaign with the slogan 'last chance to save the pound'. It was a disastrous miscalculation and perhaps a clear indication that the 1999 election to the European Parliament was perhaps not about the electorate's serious wish to express an opinion on specific aspects of government policy on Europe, but more of a

Table 9.1 Comparison of 1997 general election and 1999 Euro-election results

Party	1997 general election		1999 Euro-election	
	% votes	Seats	% votes	Seats
Labour	43.2	416	28.0	29
Conservative	30.7	165	35.8	36
Lib Dem	16.8	46	12.7	10
SNP	2.0	6	2.7	2
Plaid Cymru	0.5	4	1.8	2
UKIP	0.3	0	7.0	3
Green	0.2	0	6.2	2

General election results, 1 May 1997, House of Commons Library Research Paper 01/38, http://www.ukpolitical.info/

chance to take a shot at the EU and the government in Westminster. In any event, the 2001 Conservative general election campaign will probably go down as one of the worst in the party's history, gaining as it did a total of three extra seats on its 1997 figure.

The fact that the Conservatives came first in these elections should, however, also be seen in terms of the share of vote that it managed to achieve. The figure of 35.8 per cent was not the sort of ringing endorsement to an opposition party in mid-term. The interchange of support between the main political parties is not really the main story here, however. European elections have often been used to kick the government in Westminster and the election in 1999 seemed no different from the one in 1994.

The key area of interest in these results was the performance of the smaller parties. Clearly, the Liberal Democrats' representation in the European Parliament leapt as a result of the use of a proportional voting system. The real novelty, however, was the seats won by the Greens and the United Kingdom Independence Party (UKIP). Neither party had ever won representation in a national election before. The Greens polled 15 per cent in the 1989 European

Parliament elections (taking advantage of voters who had deserted a hopelessly divided Liberal Democrat Party at the time), but the simple plurality voting system meant that this did not materialise into seats. The Greens had been represented in countries such as the Netherlands for many years. In 1998, the party joined forces with the SPD (the centre-left social democratic party) in Germany as part of the new coalition government. In both these countries proportional electoral systems had helped the Greens win seats. In the case of Germany, which uses the additional member system of voting, the Greens were able to get representation in the **Bundestag** because of the top-up vote using the party list element of the system.

UKIP probably had more to be satisfied about. First, it won more seats than any other small party had done in previous elections to the European Parliament. Secondly, the party was relatively new and not that well known compared to parties such as the Greens that had been fighting elections since the 1980s. Finally, and perhaps most significantly, UKIP had campaigned with a message which was virtually tailor-made for the election they were fighting. The election was about the European Union, and UKIP had, and has, one fairly simple idea, which is to pull the United Kingdom out of the European Union.

The 1999 election to the European Parliament tells a number of stories. It makes clear that when a proportional voting system is used, there is likely to be more diversity in the number of parties that gain representation. Secondly, parties that have a message which is relevant to the election will do well. In the case of both the Conservatives and UKIP there appears to have been some resonance with the Euro-sceptic tone of the Conservatives and the positively anti-EU message of UKIP, which made them attractive to voters. The extent to which this means that these are not second-order elections will be explored later in the chapter. Suffice to say that Europe hardly caused a flicker on the 'policy meter' in the 2001 general election, which begs the question of just how important the issue is in the minds of voters. Perhaps the response to this question is that the salience of an issue like Europe may vary from one type of election to another.

The second elections to the European Parliament using the party list system were held five years later, in June 2004. The results of these elections are provided in Table 9.2 below.

Table 9.2 Elections to the European Parliament 2004

Party	Votes	%	Seats	Adjusted change
Conservative	4,397,087	26.7%	27	-8
Labour	3,718,683	22.6%	19	-6
UKIP	2,660,768	16.2%	12	+10
Lib Dem	2,452,327	14.9%	12	+2
Green	1,028,283	6.2%	2	0
BNP	808,201	4.9%	0	0
Respect	252,216	1.5%	0	0
SNP	231,505	1.4%	2	0
Plaid Cymru	159,888	1.0%	1	-1
Others	749,645	4.6%	0	0
Total	16,458,603	100.0%	75	-

Source: European Parliament elections 2004. House of Commons Library Research Paper 04/50.

It should be noted that the adjusted change column may appear to be at variance with the pie chart in Figure 9.2. This is because the calculation had to be made on the basis of the total number of UK seats in the European Parliament, which was reduced from eighty-seven to seventy-eight seats for these elections. The figures are for Great Britain only and exclude Northern Ireland, which uses a different voting system (STV) to elect its MEPs. (The result in Northern Ireland saw the UUP and DUP holding the single seat it had won five years earlier. The SDLP lost its only seat and Sinn Féin picked up the remaining seat.)

It is interesting to examine the change in the votes of the main parties between these two elections in Britain (excluding Northern Ireland). Table 9.3 provides this data.

The success of the smaller parties in the 1999 election was certainly built upon in 2004. These parties did particularly well in England, with a stronger performance by the British National Party,

Table 9.3 Comparison of 1999 and 2004 elections to the European Parliament

Party	1999 % votes	2004 % votes	% change
Conservative	35.8	26.7	-9.1
Labour	28.0	22.6	-5.4
Liberal Democrat	12.7	14.9	**2.2**
UKIP	7.0	16.2	**9.2**
Green	6.2	6.2	0
BNP	1.1	4.9	**3.8**
Respect	n/a	1.5	----
SNP	2.7	1.4	-1.3
Plaid Cymru	1.8	1.0	-0.8
Others	4.7	4.6	-0.1
Total	**100**	**100**	----

http://www.ukpolitical.info/ and European Parliament elections 2004, House of Commons Library Research Paper 04/50.

for example. Others, such as George Galloway's Respect Party, did not really capitalise on the unpopularity of the Blair government in the midst of the insurgency in Iraq. In any event, neither of these parties was able to convert the support it had into seats, and in the case of the BNP this amounted to over 800,000 votes.

Those smaller parties that had done well in 1999 continued to prosper. The Greens held on to their seats and UKIP was able to see its seats increase fourfold on the previous election. The following pie chart provides a more graphical representation of the distribution of UK seats in the European Parliament after the 2004 election. (Northern Ireland seats have been added for the purposes of comparison with Table 9.3 for the 1999 Euro-elections.)

It is interesting to compare the decline in the Conservative–Labour share of UK seats in the European Parliament between 1994 and 2004. Ten years previously, these parties had all but seven of the seats. By 2004, thirty-eight of these seats were held by parties other than the

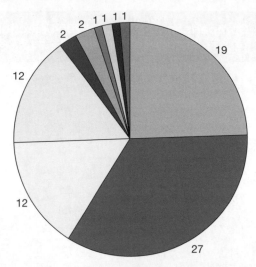

Source: European Parliament elections 2004, House of Commons Library Research Paper 04/50.

Figure 9.3 Party share of seats in the 2004 elections to the European Parliament

Conservatives and Labour. The two main parties' combined share of the seats had fallen to around 60 per cent, and, perhaps more significantly, their combined share of the vote had fallen to less than half. This is a somewhat historic point to record, because it is the first time in any national election that the combined Conservative and Labour share of the vote had failed to achieve 50 per cent. Michael Howard, the Conservative Party leader, might have proclaimed his satisfaction at the result, beating Labour into second place. In reality, these figures pointed to an even more alarming desertion of votes from the Conservatives than from Labour. The fall in the Conservative vote was almost double that of the Labour Party. In response to this point, it could be claimed that Labour had already lost a significant share of the vote in 1999 and that there was less potential for significantly greater Labour losses. The Conservatives were the main party of opposition, however, and this would be their last big electoral test before the general election. They might have hoped for a better showing than this. A more detailed analysis of the 2004 results can be found in the election study by David Butler and Martin Westlake.[2]

One of the questions asked in the previous three chapters was the extent to which voters in Scotland, Wales and Northern Ireland treated the elections to their devolved Parliament and Assembly as second-order elections. The measure that was used in Chapters 6 and 7 was to analyse the data from surveys that compared voting in real and **hypothetical elections**. One of the reasons for such analysis is to ascertain whether voting in devolved elections is to some degree a protest vote against the governing party in Westminster and that these elections constitute second-order elections. Evidence suggested that in Scotland and Wales, voters did behave differently in different types of election and that this was not simply expressing a protest vote; rather voters were voting on issues that they thought were relevant to the elections that were being contested. The analysis for Northern Ireland was complicated by the fact that there is no real way of comparing elections, given that the main UK political parties do not participate in elections in Northern Ireland. When examining differential turnout, however, it was found that there was little difference in participation levels amongst Northern Ireland voters in general elections and those for the Northern Ireland Assembly.

Attempting similar analysis for elections to the European Parliament presents a different set of challenges. As mentioned above, these elections do not result in the election of an executive body which will be making decisions in the same way as, for example, the Scottish Parliament. Furthermore, the European Parliament sits for some of its sessions in Strasbourg and others in Brussels. These places are relatively remote and it remains doubtful that many voters take an active interest in the goings-on in France and Belgium. There may be exceptions to this, however; if there is an expenses scandal in the European Parliament, the Euro-sceptic elements in the British press would no doubt be keen to report it at home.

What factors can be analysed to discover whether elections to the European Parliament are second-order in nature? In the previous chapter, electoral turnout was examined. Can any conclusions be drawn by looking at electoral turnout in general and Euro-elections? Table 9.4 offers a comparison of the turnout in general elections and elections to the European Parliament since 1979.

The figures in the table are not conclusive. There is clearly less of an incentive to turn out at elections to the European Parliament

Table 9.4	Comparison of turnout in Westminster and Euro-elections		
General election	**% turnout**	**Euro-election**	**% turnout**
1979	76.0	1979	32.7
1983	72.7	1984	32.6
1987	75.3	1989	36.8
1992	77.7	1994	36.8
1997	71.4	1999	24.0
2001	59.4	2004	38.5
2005	61.4	2009	34.7

Combined sources: http://www.ukpolitical.info/Turnout45.htm and European Parliament elections 2004, House of Commons Library Research Paper 04/50.

than at those to the House of Commons, but the picture is clouded by some complicating factors. First, turnout has fallen quite dramatically in general elections from a position consistently and comfortably above 70 per cent up until the 1992 poll, after which it declined to around 70 per cent; by the first two elections of the new millennium, the turnout had tumbled by a further 10 per cent. The differential between these latter levels of turnout and those for European elections therefore has diminished. Secondly, the turnout in Euro-elections has remained robust and, apart from the first elections using proportional representation, has seen a slight increase. This would appear to indicate that the salience of these elections has possibly increased to some extent from being very low in the 1980s.

Could the success of parties such as the Greens and UKIP as a consequence of the use of the regional party list system be the reason for the resurgence in turnout in 2004? This figure rose by 14.5 per cent between 1999 and 2004. Apart from the general election in 1918 (which saw a dramatic fall in turnout on the previous election in 1910) the 2004 elections to the European Parliament saw the biggest change in turnout between any other national elections in the country's history.

The conventional wisdom has been that Euro-elections have been second-order in nature. The trend in the turnouts would suggest otherwise. Another way to examine these elections is to analyse the pattern of party support. The results of the first four Euro-elections were masked by the workings of the simple plurality system. Seats largely changed from Labour to Conservative and back again. Liberal support fluctuated wildly during the same period, so no real conclusions can be drawn from these results.

The results of the more recent Euro-elections do provide a better profile for analysis. It is clear that a significant portion of the electorate did respond to the anti-EU message of UKIP (and, as will be seen later in the chapter, a similar message from the BNP). The Conservatives may have wanted to adopt the Euro-sceptic mantle but it was other, smaller parties who were able to capitalise on anti-European sentiment in the UK. For many hundreds of thousands of voters, therefore, these elections were not second order in nature. Disgruntled Labour supporters looking for a party to support as a protest vote could easily have chosen the Conservatives or the Liberal Democrats, as normally happens in local government elections and parliamentary **by-elections**. Instead, they chose to support a party that has existed for a relatively short time; their message being relevant to the election being fought.

It should be stressed at this point that a number of voters will choose to use elections such as these in order to protest against the government of the day in the United Kingdom. This may contradict the points made above; equally, it may reflect the reality that different motivations affect different voters and that for some voters any election other than the one to elect the UK government will be seen as a second-order election.

Much of the analysis so far has been confined to the first two elections to the European Parliament using the regional party list proportional voting system. The following section looks at the outcome of the third election, in 2009.

The performance of political parties

In the previous three chapters, this section has begun by examining the nature of the party system in Scotland, Wales and Northern Ireland respectively. In each case a four- party system was identified.

Box 9.1 The 2009 UK elections to the European Parliament

Table 9.5 provides a summary of the results of the GB elections to the European Parliament held in June 2009. The figures exclude the three seats that are allocated to Northern Ireland (once again won by the UUP, DUP and Sinn Féin).

Table 9.5 Elections to the European Parliament 2009 (excluding NI)

Party	%	Seats
Conservative	27.7%	25
Labour	15.7%	13
UKIP	16.5%	13
Lib Dem	13.7%	11
Green	8.6%	2
BNP	6.2%	2
SNP	2.1%	2
Plaid Cymru	0.8%	1

Source: Regional Returning Officers.

The following figure provides a graphic representation of the distribution of UK seats in the European Parliament following the 2009 elections.

These figures are in many ways more remarkable than those of 2004. Labour appears to be in its death throes, securing just over 15 per cent of the national vote, a record low for the party. The Conservatives, the party that most commentators believe will form the next UK government, have increased their share of the vote by only 1 per cent. They were able to secure just over one in four of the votes cast in this election. They lost two seats since 2004 (although the total number of European Parliament seats was reduced to seventy-two).

The combined Conservative and Labour share of the vote has fallen to just over 43 per cent, a new record low for a national election.

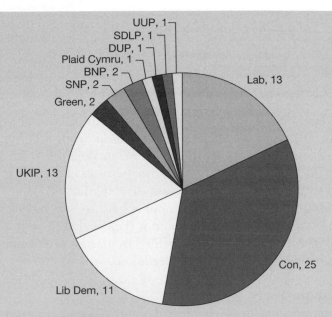

UUP, 1
SDLP, 1
DUP, 1
Plaid Cymru, 1
BNP, 2
SNP, 2
Green, 2
Lab, 13
UKIP, 13
Con, 25
Lib Dem, 11

Source: Regional Returning Officers.

Figure 9.4 Party share of seats in the 2009 UK elections to the European Parliament

This is a far cry from the early 1950s, when these two parties could command over 98 per cent of votes in a general election. The two-party system does not appear to be an appropriate description of elections to the European Parliament.

Once again, it is the performance of the smaller political parties which provides most to comment upon. The United Kingdom Independence Party has consolidated its position with a modest increase in its vote and an increase in its seats of one. The Greens, too, have held on to their seats and increased their share of the vote. The year 2009 saw the party's next best showing in a national election since the 1999 elections to the European Parliament. Perhaps the big story on the night that the election results were announced was that of the British National Party. The party polled less than it did in 2004, but the low turnout (in the main it would seem due to Labour voters staying at home) helped the BNP win its first seats in a national election. These seats were in Lancashire and Yorkshire, areas of the country where the party had been successful in local government elections. The party had campaigned against the EU labour laws that ensured equal working rights to workers from across the EU. The party succeeded to an extent in painting the picture of migrant workers from poorer EU countries coming to the UK in the midst of recession and increasing unemployment to take the jobs of British people.

In Scotland, for example, Labour, the SNP, the Conservatives and the Liberal Democrats dominated the vote in Scottish Westminster constituencies and in the Scottish Parliament. When examining elections to the European Parliament, however, most of the UK is being studied rather than a single element of it. Unlike Scotland, Wales and Northern Ireland, there does not appear to be a replication of the party system in Westminster and it is clear that there is a much greater plurality of party support for UK parties in the European Parliament than in the House of Commons.

The Labour Party

As in the previous three chapters, Labour's story has been one of decline. In 1994, the party secured sixty-four seats in the European Parliament. By 2009, it had only thirteen. Clearly, a number of factors have worked against the party. First, the proportional system was bound to have an impact on the party's representation of seats. The decline in MEPs was also due to a fall in these elections in Labour's vote, which almost halved between 1999 and 2009. The second factor worth noting is that Labour had been elected in 1997 on a platform which included a constructive dialogue with other members of the EU. During the elections to the European Parliament, more Euro-sceptic political parties are able to paint this stance as one of weakness or 'giving in to Europe'. Finally, with Labour as the governing party, many voters will choose to use these elections as a protest against those in political power.

Perhaps more worrying for the Labour Party has been the recent success of the BNP, which has prospered in the poorer working-class areas of parts of northern England that were at one time heartlands of Labour support. The BNP message of **migrant workers** from other parts of the EU coming to Britain to work at low levels of pay appeared to strike a chord with many workers facing a bleak future in the harsh economic climate of the summer of 2009.

In both the 1999 and 2004 elections to the European Parliament, Labour trailed behind the Conservatives but went on to win the subsequent general elections. In the aftermath of the 2009 debacle, a number of senior Labour politicians appeared on the news channels to make precisely this point and predict that the same will happen in 2010. The main difference between these earlier elections and those of 2009 is that then, using all other methods of gauging public opinion, Labour still outstripped the Conservatives before and after the elections. The results in 2009 gave yet further evidence that Labour was heading for defeat in 2010. In the event Labour did lose, but the Conservative victory was not that clear cut.

The Conservative Party

The Conservatives' more Euro-sceptic approach has undoubtedly been more attractive to many voters who regard the European Union with a degree of suspicion. During the Thatcher years, the party dominated these elections. Conservative support never reached the heights of 1979 and now the party has to settle with just over a quarter of the votes. The 1994 elections were a low point at the time, coming as they did during a period of growing public disenchantment with the government of John Major in the years after '**Black Wednesday**'. The 1999 elections marked a major bounce back for the party with a 9 per cent increase in its share of the vote and a doubling of its share of the seats.

Paradoxically, it was these elections that were to prove how problematic proportional representation would be for the Conservative Party. The election of 1999 also saw success for UKIP, proving that there was another force of Euro-scepticism capable of connecting with large numbers of voters. The Conservatives' vote declined by 9 per cent in 2004 (taking it to below its percentage figure when John Major was Prime Minister). UKIP's vote increased by 9 per cent, and although the dynamics of party change mean it is unlikely that there was a straight switch from the Conservatives to UKIP, there is no question that the latter did target Conservative voters during the 2004 election campaign.

Much to the relief of the Conservative Party leadership, there was a slight recovery in 2007, and the rapid rise of UKIP appears to have been halted. Other newcomers, such as the BNP, seem to be a more of a threat to Labour. The 2009 results also gave the Conservatives their biggest lead over the Labour Party in percentage votes since the first elections to the European Parliament in 1979. That poll came just five weeks after Margaret Thatcher became Prime Minister. David Cameron will be hoping that these are good omens for the next UK general election in 2010.

The Liberal Democrats

The Liberal Democrats failed to win any seats in the European Parliament until 1994, when they won two seats based on 16.2 per cent of the vote. If a proportional voting system had been used it would have won fourteen seats. Clearly, then, the introduction of the regional party list voting system for the 1999 elections was good news for the party. The party share of the seats increased fivefold in this election, proving the point the party had consistently made for the previous thirty years that a proportional electoral system would be a fairer system for all political parties.

The use of the proportional system has, however, been beneficial to other small parties, and the Liberal Democrat share of the vote is lower than it was before the introduction of the new voting system. So the party has won extra seats, but its vote has varied between 12.7 per cent and 14.9 per cent in these elections.

The Liberal Democrats undoubtedly have to limit their expectations in these elections. Forces of Euro-scepticism in the form of the Conservatives, UKIP and the BNP have been a draw on many votes over the years. Coupled with this is the Liberal Democrats' traditional pro-European stance, and their commitment to taking the pound sterling into the **Euro-zone** has left the party even more prone to sceptic attack than the Labour Party. It is interesting how the party's message towards Europe was much cooler in 2009, a reflection perhaps of the march of public opinion on the issue before and during the campaign.

United Kingdom Independence Party

It is remarkable that this party, founded only in 1993, is now the second largest UK party in the European Parliament in terms of vote, beating both Labour and the Liberal Democrats into third and fourth positions respectively. The party's history and Euro-scepticism has meant that it has had an appeal especially to those who believe that the Conservatives have become less robust in dealing with Europe since Mrs Thatcher left Downing Street at the end of 1990.

The party's initial success in the 1999 elections to the European Parliament was undoubtedly influenced by the demise of another, more visible Euro-sceptic party, the **Referendum Party**. Obviously, another important factor in UKIP's success in 1999 was the proportional voting system used. Since then, the party's support has doubled; undoubtedly success has bred success. Voters seeing a party succeed and win seats are encouraged to support the party next time round.

The party's salience has largely been confined to its performance in elections to the European Parliament. It fielded over 400 candidates in the 2001 general election, but polled only 1.5 per cent of the vote. In 2005, the figure did increase, but only to 2.2 per cent. UKIP's leader at the time was Nigel Farage. He has sought to broaden the appeal of the party beyond just the policy of withdrawal from the EU, by promoting conservative and libertarian policies, in the hope perhaps of attracting voters who may believe that David Cameron has become too much of a Tony Blair-like politician.

UKIP's hope of breaking into Westminster politics may be hampered by a number of factors, however. First, the simple plurality voting system has worked and will continue to work against political parties like UKIP. Secondly, the Conservative Party has made a major recovery from its poor standing of the late 1990s and early 2000s. Despite Farage's hopes, his party was squeezed at the 2010 general election. Overall, the 2009 Euro-election results showed some levelling off of UKIP support. It may well be that after a decade of rapid growth the party has found its ceiling, at least for the moment.

The British National Party

Formed as a splinter group of another far-right political party, the National Front, the BNP has had a number of false dawns. Its electoral successes had previously been confined to council seat victories in a number of poor urban communities in Lancashire and Yorkshire, and local government successes in places such as Barking and Dagenham in the south-east. Its performance in general elections has generally been poor. In 2005, the party secured less than 1 per cent of the vote. Although the party only came fifth in the 2008 London Mayoral election, it did secure a seat in the Greater London Assembly. In 2010 the BNP polled 1.9% of votes but won no seats.

In 2009, the BNP won two seats to the European Parliament, one in the North West region and the other in Yorkshire and the Humber. This success in the 2009 elections to the European Parliament needs to be seen in a broader context. The party's number of votes in 2009 was actually lower than in 2004 when it won no seats. The collapse of the Labour vote in the party's traditional heartlands has obviously contributed to the BNP's success in these elections.

It is difficult at this point to make any determination about the future of the BNP in European elections. The next Euro-election will be in 2014, with the next general election set for May 2015 by the coalition government's decision to move to five-year fixed-term parliaments. The key to the BNP's success is likely to be determined by the Labour Party's ability to reconnect with many of its traditional voters in places like Barnsley and Burnley.

The impact of the regional party list system

There is little doubt that the regional list system has helped smaller political parties in a manner that they have not been helped by other systems discussed in this book. The constituency elements of the additional member system and the single transferable vote have limited the scope for smaller political parties to have much more than a marginal impact on representation. The nature of the list system, with its large regional voting areas, provides relatively rich pickings for small parties. In Wales, smaller parties are significantly under-represented and in Northern Ireland there is a marginal under-representation of smaller parties.

The picture in elections to the European Parliament is completely different. In the first instance, what constitutes a minor political party in Euro-electoral terms? Not only did UKIP supplant the Liberal Democrats into fourth place in 2004, it also pushed Labour into third place in 2009, putting that party on an equal number of seats.

Between them, UKIP, the Greens and the BNP polled 31.3 per cent of the vote in the 2009 Euro-elections. Their combined share of the seats in the European Parliament represents just under 25 per cent of the total UK seats, meaning an under-representation of around six seats. The Conservatives are over-represented, also by around six seats. So clearly there is still some bias against smaller parties such as the Greens.

Despite this problem, however, there is little doubt that the sheer number of smaller party MEPs has raised the profile of these political parties in a way that has not been seen in Scotland, Wales and Northern Ireland. If this has raised the salience of the issue of Europe and the interest in elections to the European Parliament, it should be seen as a challenge to the bigger political parties not to take the electorate for granted and to connect with voters on the issues about which they feel strongly.

What you should have learnt from reading this chapter

- The background to elections to the European Parliament
- An understanding of the basis of voting behaviour in elections to the European Parliament
- The main similarities and differences between elections to the European Parliament and to Westminster
- The results of the three elections to the European Parliament using proportional representation
- The fortunes of the political parties in elections to the European Parliament
- The use of the regional party list used for elections to the European Parliament

Glossary of key terms

Black Wednesday The name given by the press to the day in September 1992 that Britain's currency was forced out of the European Exchange Rate Mechanism (ERM). The value of the pound was stabilised at around three Deutsche Marks. The various central banks of all the EU states in the ERM would maintain this level (within a band of tolerance). On Black Wednesday, speculative pressure forced the pound to lose 15 per cent of its value and the central banks failed to halt the slide. The government of John Major was blamed for economic incompetence and the government never regained its loss of public support.

Bundestag The name of the lower House of Parliament in Germany. It is the equivalent of the House of Commons in the United Kingdom.

By-election In Britain, an election that takes place in a constituency where a vacancy has arisen due to either the death, resignation or disqualification of a Member of Parliament or other elected representative.

Euro-sceptic A term used to describe those people who have a negative attitude towards the institutions and policies of the European Union. During John Major's premiership there was a significant Euro-sceptic wing within the Conservative Party, with a number of Euro-sceptic MPs, such as Michael Portillo and John Redwood, sitting in the Cabinet. The term is, however, not necessarily restricted to Conservative critics of the EU.

Euro-zone The group of European Union countries that use the euro as their currency. The UK has not been involved in the process of monetary union after obtaining an opt-out of the Maastricht Treaty in 1992. Since then there has been intense debate about whether the UK should join the Euro-zone. The Conservatives have effectively ruled it out forever and Labour, having said it would apply certain tests about the UK's readiness for the single currency before having a referendum on the subject, has abandoned all thought of joining.

Hypothetical election This is not a real election. Public opinion bodies often ask the question, 'If there were a general election held tomorrow, which party would you support?' The studies cited in previous chapters asked voters who had participated in elections to the Scottish Parliament and the National Assembly for Wales to declare how they would have voted if there had been a general election held at the same time. Voters in Wales who had participated in a general election were also asked to declare how they would have voted if there had been an election to the National Assembly for Wales held at the same time.

Migrant workers People who choose to look abroad for work. Many migrant workers from those countries who have recently joined the European Union (such as Poland or the Baltic states) have come to the UK where there are better-paid job opportunities. Many UK citizens are also migrant workers, that is to say they have gone abroad to other EU countries in order to find employment.

Referendum Party The party set up by the multi-millionaire businessman Sir James Goldsmith. The party had broadly Euro-sceptic views and, as its name suggests, it wanted a referendum on Britain's future position in Europe (although it remained vague, in public at least, about how the referendum question would be worded). The party fielded candidates in the 1997 general election in constituencies where candidates refused to endorse Goldsmith's call for a referendum. Although the party had an impact on a number of constituency results (usually taking votes from Conservative candidates), it won no seats.

Reunification Following the fall of the Berlin Wall in October 1989 and the collapse of the East German Communist system, West Germany and East Germany were unified into one single sovereign entity in 2000. This turned Germany into the most populous country in the European Union. **Second-order elections** A term used to describe elections where voters might choose to use a protest vote against the government in Westminster. Local council elections or elections to the European Parliament are often described as such. If voters are seen to vote in a devolved election on the basis of devolved rather than UK-wide issues and differently to the way they would in a general election, then the elections concerned would not be described as second-order elections.

Likely examination questions

Account for the changes in support for political parties fighting elections to the European Parliament.

'Results from the recent elections to the European Parliament show that the British two-party system is dead.' Discuss.

Helpful websites

BBC European Parliament results webpages

http://news.bbc.co.uk/1/shared/bsp/hi/elections/euro/09/html/ukregion_999999.stm

European Parliament elections webpages

http://www.europarl.org.uk/section/european-elections/european-elections

Suggestions for further reading

M. Bruter and Y. Déloye, *Encyclopedia of European Elections*, Macmillan, 2007.

D. Butler and M. Westlake, *British Politics and European Elections, 1999*, Palgrave Macmillan, 2000.

W. van der Brug and C. van der Eijk (eds), *European Elections and Domestic Politics: Lessons from the Past and Scenarios for the Future*, University of Notre Dame Press, 2007.

Conclusion

Contents

Overview

Voting behaviour in the UK has changed dramatically over the past sixty years. An era of stable, aligned voting has given way to a period of volatility. The workings of the simple plurality electoral system have to some extent masked the full extent of voter volatility in recent decades.

This chapter examines the extent to which voter volatility has now become more fully manifest with the introduction of different electoral systems across the UK.

Key issues to be covered in this chapter

* Conclusions on voting behaviour in UK general elections
* An assessment of the different electoral systems used in the UK
* An overview of how the main political parties have fared with these different electoral systems
* An assessment of the impact of these electoral systems

Voting behaviour

Britain in the past was defined by political stability. In the 1950s and 1960s, the Conservative and Labour parties dominated politics in the country. The impact of third parties in national politics was largely peripheral, to the point of virtual irrelevance. The old alignments of social class and party identification were the main determinants of how most people voted. These alignments were not perfect fits and they did not prevent political change from taking place. There were changes of government, but these tended to be based on very modest and uniform swings of political support across the country.

After 1970, it would appear that many of the certainties of these earlier decades started to exhibit signs of weakening, although it is clear from such research as Crewe et al. (1977) that some of the forces which were responsible for this were at work before 1970. The once strong two-party dominance was being broken; the Conservative and Labour combined share of the vote was in significant decline. The main causes of this decline were largely due to the weakening of both partisanship and the influence of social class.

These shifts of support away from Conservative and Labour did not benefit other political parties, who were unable to make the political inroads that one might have expected. The Liberal Party did not see any meaningful reward from polling over six million votes in 1974. Labour was still able to cling to power in the late 1970s, despite having no parliamentary majority, and after 1979, the two parties would have long periods in office with their shares of the vote heading in a downward trajectory. Some smaller parties have done better; the Scottish National Party was able to make a big impact north of the border in the 1970s. But for third parties, fielding candidates nationwide and amassing millions of votes, there was no tangible reward in terms of seats in the House of Commons. The nature of the electoral system was largely responsible for this situation and from then on it came in for sustained criticism.

Different electoral systems

In examining different electoral systems, the first part of this book discussed a number of themes. As well as explaining the workings of the systems and their main consequences, an assessment of each system in terms of its impact on governance and representation was also provided. One reason for maintaining the simple plurality system is because it is easy to understand, it maintains political stability and it seems to result in strong government, with the result that governments remain in power long enough to enact their manifesto promises. On the other hand, the simple plurality system produces governments that have manifestos but no real electoral mandate to enact policies. There has not been a single government elected to Westminster since 1945 that has had a majority of the popular vote. This trend is getting worse; in 2005 Labour won its third successive election with just over a third of the vote.

Majoritarian electoral systems have been used both in the UK and elsewhere in the world to overcome the problem of MPs being elected without a majority of votes. The second ballot effectively operates by a process of elimination. If no candidate receives a majority of votes in the first ballot, then a second is held between the top two candidates. The alternative vote and the supplementary vote achieve a similar outcome using one ballot, but in these systems, voters express their preferences for different candidates. If no candidate gets over half of the first-preference votes, the candidate with the fewest is eliminated and those votes are redistributed to the remaining candidates. This continues until one candidate is elected with over 50 per cent of the votes. The problem with both these systems is that they do not ensure that the government is elected with 50 per cent of the vote and, as such, these are not the preferred systems of groups such as the Electoral Reform Society, which favour proportional electoral systems.

Proportional electoral systems result in a proportional relationship between the number of votes obtained by a party and the seats it receives in an assembly. The party list system simply involves candidates choosing a party. The total vote for any party will determine the seats it receives; MPs are then allocated from the various party lists. The problem with this system is that it effectively severs the link between the MP and the constituent. For this reason it will probably never be a realistic alternative for use in elections to the House of Commons. Its use in UK elections to the European Parliament has led to a major increase in the representation of smaller political parties, such as the Greens and the United Kingdom Independence Party. The single transferable vote maintains the MP–constituent link by having multi-member electoral districts, with voters expressing a preference for the candidates. To be elected, candidates must reach a quota, and votes in excess of this quota are reallocated to other candidates. If no candidate reaches the quota, then the lowest-placed candidate is eliminated and the votes reallocated (as with the alternative vote). The Liberal Democrats and the Electoral Reform Society would like to see this voting system introduced for elections to the House of Commons, but this is unlikely to happen given the size of the multi-member constituencies required and the relative complexity of the system. It is, however, now used for elections to the Northern Ireland Assembly. In a divided community such as Northern Ireland, the STV's multi-member electoral districts have provided the opportunity for representatives from more than one of the political and religious traditions to be elected in the same constituency. The additional member system is a hybrid, a combination of the simple plurality system and the party list system. Proportionality is achieved by additional members from the list being combined with the winners of the simple plurality elections in the constituencies. One of the criticisms of this voting system is that it creates a two-tier system of MPs; one which represents constituencies, and another which has no constituency link, and thus a less direct line of accountability. The system is now used to elect the Scottish Parliament, the National Assembly for Wales and the Greater London Assembly. Both Scotland and Wales have seen coalition government as a result of this electoral system being used.

In the later chapters in this book a number of questions were posed about the politics of the institutions that are now elected using proportional electoral systems. First, how do voting patterns compare between these elections to the devolved assemblies and the European Parliament, and elections to the House of Commons? Secondly, are these other elections second-order elections, in other words are they treated less seriously than elections to Westminster? Which political parties have done well and less well out of the use of these electoral systems? Is there evidence to show that the use of one proportional voting system produces a different outcome to another proportional system?

Comparing elections

In the case of both the Scottish Parliament and the National Assembly for Wales there appeared to be clear differences in the outcomes of these elections and those to the House of Commons. In particular, the performance of the nationalist parties was consistently higher in elections to the devolved assemblies than it was to Westminster elections. In both countries Labour's dominance has been eroded by nationalist forces to the extent that even when the party has been in power, on no occasion did it achieve over half of the seats in either assembly. Indeed, no party has won an election with a majority of seats in either Scotland or Wales in any of the devolved elections.

Northern Ireland presents a difficult comparative exercise, if only because the main Westminster political parties do not compete in elections in Northern Ireland, and consequently it is very difficult to make a meaningful comparison. The main conclusions to be drawn are really relevant to later sections of this chapter examining the fortunes of the political parties and the impact of the single transferable vote electoral system.

In comparing the UK elections to those to the European Parliament and the House of Commons, an increasingly divergent pattern of party distribution emerges. In each successive Euro-election we see an increased representation of parties other than the Conservatives and Labour, with the two parties barely holding on to a majority of seats between them. By 2004, the two-party share of the vote had fallen to below 50 per cent, the first time this had occurred in a national election. In the 2005 general election, this figure was well above 60 per cent.

Second-order elections

It is tempting to see all elections other than those to the House of Commons as less important. After all, in a unitary state such as the United Kingdom, most power does flow from the party that has the majority of House of Commons seats. Yet the indications that voters might use the elections to the devolved assemblies and the European Parliament as mere protest votes are not borne out on closer scrutiny. Voters in elections to the Scottish Parliament and the National Assembly for Wales seemed to be aware of the distinct issues at stake in these elections and in elections to the House of Commons. Survey data showed that many voters would change the way they had voted in an assembly election if there were a hypothetical general election held. Both the Scots and the Welsh, it would appear, vote on the merits of the issues that matter in the election itself and do not appear to confuse issues between elections. This, of course, will not be true of all electors in devolved elections. There are still bound to be some who do use elections such as these to punish the governing party in Westminster.

Northern Ireland does pose a problem of comparison for the reasons outlined in the previous section. When looking at electoral turnout, however, it can be seen that at a time when UK turnout was falling in general elections, voting in Northern Ireland was higher than the UK average and that in the case of elections to the Northern Ireland Assembly, turnout has actually exceeded that in the general election. Once again, there is an indication that voters are treating the issues in these elections seriously.

It may be suggested that of all of the elections examined in this book, those to the European Parliament are those most likely to qualify as second-order elections. In both 1999 and 2004, the Labour Party was dealt a heavy blow by voters in these elections, only to be re-elected in the following general election. This may be described as the classic sign of a protest vote. In addition, turnout in these elections has been very low, again indicating that voters do not take these elections seriously.

More careful analysis, however, reveals that a different picture is emerging. In the first instance, while turnout remains low, it has actually remained fairly steady over the past ten years at a time when voting in general elections has fallen alarmingly. It may be that the success of parties such as UKIP and the Greens has ignited interest in elections where, at one time, only Labour and the Conservatives had a chance of winning a seat. The very success of parties such as UKIP also confirms that a great many voters do have a firm view on the issue of Europe and are prepared to register their vote accordingly.

The political parties

As mentioned above, the main parties to benefit in elections to the Scottish Parliament and the Welsh National Assembly have been the

nationalists. They have effectively become the main parties of opposition and in 2007, they achieved even more. The SNP became the
minority government in Scotland and Plaid Cymru has a share of
government (with the Welsh Labour Party) in Wales. For the Liberal
Democrats, it has been a picture of mixed fortunes, having been the
coalition partners in Scotland between 1999 and 2007, but failing to
make any further inroads in Wales.

In Northern Ireland there has been a polarisation of political
support in the province. The more moderate forces of unionism and
nationalism, the UUP and the SDLP respectively, have lost ground to
the more extreme parties, the DUP and Sinn Féin. This is not a phenomenon particular to elections to the Northern Ireland Assembly,
however; the same forces appear to be at work in both elections to
the House of Commons and in Northern Ireland's elections to the
European Parliament.

In the elections to the European Parliament, the big picture is
about the smaller parties who have increased their share of the vote
and seats over the past decade. In earlier times, the Conservative
Party would have been the traditional home for the more Euro-
sceptic voter. The party has struggled to maintain its share of the
vote in recent elections as the United Kingdom Independence Party
has seen its support increase to a position where in 2009, the party
came second in terms of share of the vote (pushing Labour into
third place). Labour, too, has something to worry about with smaller
political parties. The success of the BNP in what should be Labour
strongholds, winning two seats in the European Parliament, will lead
to much party soul-searching about how to reconnect with some of
its traditional voters.

The impact of the voting systems

It is clear from analysis in the previous four chapters that the voting
systems used in the devolved and European elections did make a
difference to the outcomes of these polls. Of course, one can make
the general point that a proportional voting system is bound to
redistribute seats in a more proportional manner. There is, however,
evidence to suggest that the different voting systems have led to different outcomes.

In the case of the elections to the Scottish Parliament and the National Assembly for Wales, it would appear that in the main the redistribution of seats took place among the existing four main parties. The main losers were the Labour Party and the main winners were the nationalists. Smaller parties made only minor inroads in both countries. In the case of Scotland, this did not amount to much of an under-representation of smaller political parties. The results from Wales, however, suggest that smaller parties should have done much better than they did. This perhaps suggests that the variant of the additional member system as operated in Wales (where only twenty of the sixty seats make up the proportional element) is insufficiently proportional. One of the main points made to justify the use of proportional representation is that it represents more political parties more fairly.

In Northern Ireland, the smaller unionist parties did particularly well in the 1998 Assembly elections. The number of smaller-party Assembly members has reduced in recent years, but so has their percentage of the vote. It is true that there is still some under-representation of smaller political parties in the Northern Ireland Assembly but this is not on the scale of what has happened in Wales.

The most important consequence of the single transferable vote is that it enables cross-party representation within the multi-member constituencies, which in a community still scarred from the divisions of the past and where inter-community suspicions still loom large, is a very important factor.

It is perhaps in elections to the European Parliament where the greatest differences may be observed. As was mentioned in Chapter 4, the party list voting system is about as pure a system of proportional representation as can be achieved (although this is somewhat blunted by the breaking-up of the country into regions, which may account for the continued over-representation of the larger political parties). Parties that have never been close to national representation have been able to win seats in the European Parliament and the number of MEPs from these parties has grown with each election since the first use of the regional party list system in 1999. As mentioned earlier in this chapter, this is one of the original reasons why this electoral system was considered unsuitable as a replacement for the simple plurality system in elections to the House of Commons. It is clear, three elections later, that another outcome, one more deadly to the two main political parties, could also accompany the introduction of this voting system to elect the Westminster Parliament.

This book has tried to examine the manner in which voting behaviour and the debate about electoral reform have been intertwined over the past forty years. It has also attempted to analyse the link between voting behaviour and the electoral systems that have been introduced for the devolved and European Parliament elections since 1997.

There is no doubt that in the first of these areas, the processes of partisan and class dealignment since the 1970s have highlighted the shortcomings of the simple plurality electoral system. The manifest unfairness to parties such as the Liberal Democrats certainly helped to increase the volume of calls for its reform, which were finally heeded by the Blair government as the twentieth century drew to a close. This response was largely predicated on the introduction of proportional electoral systems for the new devolved assemblies.

The use of these electoral systems in the devolved assemblies and in elections to the European Parliament has, if anything, further loosened voters' ties to the Conservative and Labour parties. In all the elections discussed in this book – those to the devolved assemblies in Scotland, Wales and Northern Ireland, to the elections to the European Parliament, even those to the House of Commons – the Conservative and Labour share of the votes has declined. It would seem that the simple plurality system is all that maintains these two parties in their position of continued control of United Kingdom politics, at least as far as elections to the House of Commons is concerned. Further reform of the UK political system does now seem to be on the agenda. The predicted stalemate in the House of Commons arrived in May 2010. No party had an overall majority to govern, and the Liberal Democrats were in a position to broker a deal with either the Conservatives or Labour. The price that the Liberal Democrats demanded for such a deal was electoral reform. Both Labour and the Conservatives offered a referendum on the alternative vote. If the British people vote to change the voting system, British politics will be changed forever.

References

Chapter 2

1. Harold Wilson, *The Labour Government 1964–1970: A Personal Record*, Weidenfeld & Nicolson, 1971, p. 174.
2. D. Butler (ed.), *Coalitions in British Politics*, Macmillan, 1978, p. 113.
3. The Plant Report: a working party on electoral reform, *The Guardian*, 1991.
4. *The Report of the Independent Commission on the Voting System*. Cm 4090-I, HMSO, 1998.

Chapter 3

1. The Plant Report: a working party on electoral reform, *The Guardian*, 1991.
2. D. Farrell, *Comparing Electoral Systems*, Prentice Hall/Harvester Wheatsheaf, 1997, pp. 40–1.
3. D. B. Godley, 'The French General Election of 21–28 March 1993', *Electoral Studies*, vol. 12, no. 4, Elsevier, 1993, pp. 291–314.
4. D. Farrell, *Comparing Electoral Systems*, Prentice Hall/Harvester Wheatsheaf, 1997, pp. 40–1.

Chapter 4

1. D. Farrell, *Comparing Electoral Systems*, Prentice Hall/Harvester Wheatsheaf, 2001.
2. P. Dunleavy, H. Margetts and S. Weir, 'Replaying the 1992 general election: how Britain would have voted under alternative electoral systems', LSE Public Policy Paper, no. 3, 1992, p.10.
3. *The Report of the Independent Commission on the Voting System*. Cm 4090-I, HMSO, 1998.

Chapter 5

1. Viscount Bryce, *Modern Democracies*, Macmillan, 1921, pp. 168–9.

2. A. Campbell, P. Converse, W. Miller and D. Stokes, *The American Voter*, John Wiley & Sons, Inc., 1960, p. 183.

3. D. Butler and D. Stokes, *Political Change in Britain*, Macmillan Press, 1974, p. 281.

4. D. Denver, *Elections and Voting Behaviour in Britain*, Prentice Hall/Harvester Wheatsheaf, 1994, pp. 31–2.

5. P. Pulzer, *Political Representation and Elections in Britain*, George Allen & Unwin, 1975, p. 109.

6. R. Samuel, 'The Deference Voter', *New Left Review*, vol. 1, Jan.–Feb. 1960, p. 11.

7. P. Pulzer, *Political Representation and Elections in Britain*, George Allen & Unwin, 1975, p. 98.

8. A. Campbell, P. Converse, W. Miller and D. Stokes, *The American Voter*, John Wiley & Sons, Inc., 1960.

9. D. Butler and D. Stokes, *Political Change in Britain*, Macmillan Press, 1974, p. 40.

10. I. Crewe, B. Sarlvik and J. Alt, 'Partisan Dealignment in Britain 1964–1974', *British Journal of Political Science*, vol. 7, no. 2, 1977, pp. 129–90.

11. I. Crewe, in I. Crewe and D. Denver, *Electoral Change in Western Democracies*, Croom Helm, 1985, p. 139.

12. D. Denver, *Elections and Voting Behaviour in Britain*, Prentice Hall/Harvester Wheatsheaf, 1994, pp. 63–4.

13. P. Norris, *Electoral Change since 1945*, Blackwell, 1997, pp. 108–14.

14. D. Denver, 'The 1997 general election results: lessons for teachers', *Talking Politics*, vol. 10, no. 1, Autumn 1997, pp. 2–8.

Chapter 6

1. L. Paterson, A. Brown, J. Curtice and K. Hinds, *New Scotland, New Politics*, Edinburgh University Press, 2002, p. 11.

2. R. Wyn Jones and R. Scully, 'Devolution and Electoral Politics in Scotland and Wales', *Publius: The Journal of Federalism*, vol. 36, no. 1, pp. 115–34, Oxford University Press.

3. P. Norris, *Electoral Change since 1945*, Blackwell, 1997.

4. R. Johns, C. Carman and D. Denver, *Problem elections, process evaluations, and willingness to vote: The impact of the Scottish election in 2007*, Scottish Election Study, University of Strathclyde, 2008, p. 12.

5. C. Carmen, J. Mitchell and R. Johns, 'The unfortunate natural experiment in ballot design: the Scottish Parliamentary Elections of 2007', *Electoral Studies*, vol. 27, no. 3, pp. 442–59, 2008.

Chapter 7

1. The National Assembly for Wales elections 2007. Report by the Electoral Commission, 2007.
2. J. Osmond, *Crossing the Rubicon: Coalition Politics Welsh Style*, Institute of Welsh Affairs, 2007.

Chapter 9

1. D. Butler and M. Westlake, *British Politics and European Elections 1999*, Palgrave Macmillan, 2000.
2. D. Butler and M. Westlake, *British Politics and European Elections 2004*, Palgrave Macmillan, 2005.

Index

Bold indicates that the term is defined